The Bumpy Road

Farm Life in the Great Depression

QUENTIN F. VEIT

edited by Ellen M. Meyer

WillowBend
PRESS

Published by Willow Bend Press

Previously published as *History of Henry Joseph Mertens and his wife Maria Magdalena Loethen (Appendix 20: The Way It Was)* in 2002

ISBN-13: 979-8-6509-7904-3

Cover design by Ellen M. Meyer and Vicki Lesage

Table of Contents

Preface

WHEN DAD FIRST STARTED WORKING on what turned out to be many genealogical books, I was not exactly enthusiastic. Yes, I bought the books, flipped through a few pages, then put them on a shelf, never to be read. They had no relevance or meaning to me at that time; the people might have been related to me, but I couldn't relate to them. They were just names in a book, and I couldn't understand what fascinated Dad about them.

But when Ellen found this book in the appendix of one of Dad's genealogies, the light bulb went on. What so fascinated Dad was learning, understanding and appreciating the way his (our) ancestors lived their lives. What excited him was not a list of names in a census, but that tidbit of a letter written during some long-ago war, or that will that listed possessions and heirs, or that bill of sale for some now-obsolete item (for what we would consider a ridiculously low price!).

All these were clues to how these people led their lives, what was important to them, what struggles they overcame, what successes they achieved. From these clues, Dad could form a picture and these people became real to him (and hopefully to his readers too.)

In the same way, this book is an attempt to make real to the readers my dad and an entire generation of Depression-era farmers. This way of life is gone now; farmers have electricity, huge gas- or diesel-fueled tractors and threshers and balers and other equipment never dreamed of back then, the dairy farmers have robotic milking machines, they all have Internet and the ability to order their seed and supplies on-line and delivered to their farms. But it's important for us all to realize the sacrifices and struggles that our ancestors went through so that we could live the lives we have today.

I believe that Dad's interest in genealogy was sparked by his intense respect and love for family. What he discovered in his painstaking research about our ancestors, he wanted to pass on to his descendants about his own life. What a wonderful legacy!

And we're excited to share that legacy with you.

In this book, you will discover the many facets of running a "Farm", how chores were done in the "Home", the importance of "Family", and the many things that tied the "Community" together and kept it close. Marvel at the strength, endurance and ingenuity of these people, be grateful that you don't have to do things that way anymore (I know I am!), and enjoy these tales of a time gone by.

Janice (Veit) Vail
April, 2020

P. S. About the title: "The Bumpy Road" is the nickname we children gave to the thinly-graveled, rutted country lane that led to our grandparents' farm. After a long drive from the city, we knew that once we left the smooth blacktop and felt those inevitable bumps through the station wagon's suspension, we were only minutes away from our destination. The farm was a grandchild's paradise: cousins to play with, trees to climb, haybale-houses to build, woods to explore, blackberries to pick, fried eggs and sausage to eat for breakfast, "Ghost in the Graveyard" to play at night.

For our dad, growing up during the Great Depression, it was not quite so heavenly. For his family and the other farmers in the community, "the bumpy road" was more the story of their lives, enduring the ups and downs and rough passage through those hard years. But after traveling that "bumpy road" they too arrived at their destination: a better life for themselves and their descendants (us!)

Introduction

THIS WRITE-UP was always intended as an appendix to the Mertens book. I decided to make copies available for reading at the Veit family reunion in 2001 because I thought there might be interest in how things were when I was young. My brother Clarence wanted to buy one but I said they were not finished and not for sale at the time. Would you believe that he won a copy as a prize?

I first got the inspiration for the appendix when I read a book sent to me by a Mertens relative, Raymond Backes of California, who was raised in Osage County, Missouri. In it he included some of his childhood memories so that, as he said, they would not be lost to posterity. I decided that I ought to do the same. The result is this appendix.

Quentin F. Veit
27 February 2002

FARM

Plowing

BEFORE PLANTING CROPS, it was necessary to first plow the ground. This was in the days before "no till" farming. Plowing was done with a ten-inch, horse-drawn plow. The plow turned over the ground at a depth of about eight to 10 inches, making a furrow about 10 inches wide. A team of two horses was used to pull the plow, with one horse walking in the furrow created on the previous pass. If you had a smart horse like we had, namely old Barney, he would push against the horse walking in the furrow, moving him over toward the plowed ground. This caused the plow to turn over a narrower strip of ground and made it easier to pull.

There were two kinds of plows, a regular plow and a chill plow. Actually, there was a third kind of plow, which was seldom used, called the new-ground plow. The regular plow had a long point and a long curving moldboard to turn over the soil. This plow had two handles which the operator used to guide the plow while he walked behind it between the handles. On some plows there was a coulter, which consisted of a rolling disk, about 12 inches in diameter and capable of swiveling, fastened to the beam of the plow. This coulter cut the ground ahead of the plow point making the plow easier to pull. The lines to the horses were fastened together and looped around the operator's waist. The horses were guided by twisting one's body.

Plowing with Horses

The operator was always in some danger of injury because there was a cross bar between the two handles. This bar would intercept the operator's rib cage if the plow came to a sudden stop such as when running into a stump or a big boulder. At the end of a furrow, the plow would have to be dragged around to head in the new direction. No kid could lift a plow so the turning around was done by lifting on the handles to raise the plow out of the ground, causing the front part of the beam to rest on the ground to act as a fulcrum point. The plow was then carried by the handles around this pivot point.

Regular Moldboard Plow Without Coulter

The regular plow was always used on the ordinary ground when the moisture conditions in the ground were right. The ground would then be lifted up by the plow point and flow ("scour") along the moldboard as it was turned over. This would leave the moldboard as bright and shiny as a mirror. Under these conditions the plow was easy for the horses to pull.

In certain types of clay soil or if moisture conditions were not right the ground would not scour along the moldboard of the ordinary plow. The ground would then stick to the plow and break up ahead of the plow, making the plow very hard for the horses to pull. In such a case the second type of plow, called a chill plow, was used. This plow had a much shorter point and a much shorter and steeper moldboard. The too-wet, or clay soil, would scour along this type of plow.

The point and edges of the share of either plow would dull with use and become hard to pull. The plowshare (front part including the point) of both types of plows was replaceable. However, it was cheaper to have a new point welded onto the plowshare of the ordinary plow by a blacksmith and to sharpen the plowshare of the chill plow. The share of the ordinary plow was ductile steel while that of the chill plow was cast iron. The chill plowshare could be sharpened by chipping the edge with a hammer much as Indians made arrow heads.

The new-ground plow was used to plow "new ground" on which trees had recently been removed. Instead of a coulter the share was preceded by a vertical curved blade fastened to the beam of the plow. This blade was curved in the reverse shape of a scimitar and its purpose was to cut roots ahead of the plow. It didn't do a thing for stumps which were "hell" for the child operator. Yes, by the time we were 12 or so we were considered big enough to plow. If the plow ran into a stump, the sharp point would lodge in or under the stump, of course stopping the horses. The child operator, who could barely lift the plow anyhow, had to work the plow loose and pull it back from the stump. A smart horse, such as our Barney, would wait until the operator had the plow almost loose and would then pull forward, lodging the plow in the stump again. This gave Barney some more time to rest, but led to much "cussing" by the poor fellow handling the plow.

Plowing was done in the summertime so we always did it walking barefoot. One time when I was plowing, walking in the furrow behind the plow barefoot, I felt something bump against my sole. As I turned to look back, I could see a snake crawling out of a hole that I had just plowed over. I didn't even bother finding out what kind of snake it was.

A dangerous, but fun thing, was to walk in the plowed land just behind the horses and ahead of the plow and stick our feet in the furrow and have the plow turn the ground over top of them. One slip of the plow and a foot could have been severely cut.

I took the trouble to calculate how far one would walk, not counting turning around at the end of a furrow, to plow an acre of ground with a 10-inch plow and it comes to 9.9 miles. In a good day, in good ground, one could plow two acres. Plowing land for 20 acres of wheat would amount to walking about 200 miles. No wonder we stayed in shape!

Fence Posts and Fencing

DAD'S FARM had a half mile of fence north and about a quarter of a mile south of the county road that ran in front of the house. Additionally it had a quarter mile on each side on the east and west borders and another half mile at the north boundary and about a quarter mile at the south boundary. This amounted to about three and a half miles of fence. With a fence post every 10 feet this took about 1800 posts for the fence, not counting separate enclosures such as the hog pasture and the barn lot.

Six-Foot Crosscut Saw

When I was around 12, it came time to replace a large number of these posts, since the bottom end in the ground would rot off or be eaten by termites after a period of years. Treated posts were unheard of at that time. That winter, almost every afternoon when I came home from school, Dad and I would go out into the woods in the "holler" behind the big field and cut down oak trees to make fence posts. A "holler" is a narrow valley with a creek in it. The trees would have to be around 12 to 16 inches in diameter. We would cut down the trees using first an axe to cut a notch on the side of the tree in the direction it would fall, and then our six-foot long, crosscut saw to cut across the backside and fell the tree. We then blocked the trunks up into six-foot lengths. With the limbs starting about 20 feet up on the trunks, we would get three post lengths out of each tree. We then used wedges and a sledgehammer to split these lengths into fence posts. A 12-inch diameter block would yield eight posts and a 16-inch diameter block would yield 12 fence posts.

That year we made a little more than 1000 posts, which required about 100 blocks or 35 trees. We cut the upper part of the trees into fire wood for the kitchen and heating stoves. We hauled the firewood lengths and posts up to an open area up the road from the house. Hauling the shorter lengths of the posts required "short-coupling" the wagon. The wagon was equipped with a coupling pole which tied the front axle and rear axles together. The coupling pole had holes in it which allowed the axles to be moved closer or further apart. A long length was used when the 20-foot hay frame was on the wagon and shorter lengths for hauling wood or logs when the hay frame was not used. The wood coupling pole was always made of hickory which would give quite a bit before it would break.

Typical Fence Post

We used Uncle George's engine-driven saw to sharpen the posts, cutting three or four triangular slabs off the posts at one end. We racked these pointed posts in a crib fashion, with 12 posts or so to a layer, near the road. Our new administrator-priest, Father Leo Oligschlager, saw these and decided that he needed 110 of them to fence in the parish grounds. Needless to say we donated them.

16-Pound Post Maul

When it came to installing the posts, we used a heavy (to a kid) punch bar, an inch and a half diameter steel rod, six feet long, to first punch a hole in the ground. The rod was jammed into the ground and then worked back and forth to enlarge the hole. The pointed end of the post was then stuck in the hole and the post was driven in with a 16-pound post maul, quite a thing to swing time after time to drive in a fence post. The posts were driven in to a depth of about one and a half feet. Since the post stood out of the ground about five feet when it was first put in the hole, it was virtually impossible to hit the top with the maul then. So we stood on a wagon to drive the post in. It was fascinating, when someone was driving a post a quarter-mile away, to hear the sound of the maul hitting the post and see the driver already swinging the maul for the next hit. This phenomenon occurred because it took sound a second to travel the 1000 feet.

Barbed Wire

Mostly we used barbed wire (pronounced "bob wire" by us) for fencing and usually four or five strands along the fence. We used a miniature block and tackle to stretch the barbed wire, one strand at a time. This could be a dangerous task because we couldn't afford new barbed wire and the old barbed wire had a tendency to break occasionally when it was stretched and then lifted off the ground to be tacked to a post with staples ("steeples" to us). If you had the wire in your hand, it would zip through your grasp and leave nasty gashes in the palm of your hand. Hence, after the wire was stretched, we would carefully pick it up using the claws of a hammer to hold it while we pulled it to the post.

On a few parts of the fencing we used woven wire at the lower part with a couple of barbed wire strands above it. We generally used the woven wire where we needed to fence in pigs because the pigs would squeeze in between any barbed wire.

Closed Ring, Open Ring, Ringer Ready for Action

This brings up an interesting thing about pigs. A pig was born to root with its nose in the dirt and would root under any fence, including the woven wire, and push out of its enclosure. To prevent this, we would put rings in the pigs' noses. The rings came in the form of an open triangle with two beveled pointy ends. These were held in a pliers-like device which, when squeezed, would bend the metal to close the triangle and drive the pointy ends through the pig's nose.

Hog Snooter

Occasionally, on some pigs, rings had to also be inserted through the skin above the nose. When this didn't work, and there were times when it didn't, a hog snooter was used.

Snooted Hog

This device cut a slit in the top of the hog's nose and a little bit around the rim of the hog's nose. I have one of these devices. It is called "Never Root" and was patented in 1900.

Janice Veit in Front of Grandma's Fence

So much for the utilitarian fencing. The decorative fencing around the yard at the house was something else. Shortly after World War II, when metal became available again, Mom decided that the woven wire fence around the yard had to be replaced. However, she did not design any old ordinary fence. A trench was dug along the whole length of the fence and a concrete wall level with the ground was poured in the trench with metal fence posts set in the concrete as were the corner braces. The front gate to the road, which had been in front of the house, was moved to the side where the driveway was. This old front gate had been there so long that a deep trench had been worn between the fence posts there. This ground was all leveled before the concrete wall was poured. The fence itself was a decorative heavy metal wire design with round top loops and was bought from Montgomery Wards or Sears.

There were some neat aspects to this fence. The most important to me was that, because of the concrete wall, no grass grew under the fence so no trimming was required when the lawn was mowed. Another was the fact that with the posts set in a concrete wall, they did not move with freezing or thawing nor did the corner braces move so the fence stayed taut and upright as the day it was installed. All of the fence would still be standing except that the front part had to be moved when the road was widened for blacktopping. The other parts of the fence stand in their pristine glory today almost 60 years after it was first installed.

Hauling Manure

WHAT WAS MANURE? There were several kinds: cow manure, horse manure, straw pile manure, and chicken manure. Cow manure was a mixture of hay that the cows pulled out of the manger when eating, straw used as bedding, and just plain old cow poop. Where was cow manure found? It was found in the stable in the barn. It collected in the stable, mostly in the wintertime when the cows were fed hay because there was no pasture available.

Of course, it had to be disposed of somehow. And that is where the manure spreader came into play. The manure spreader had four wheels, two smaller ones in the front that turned with the tongue, two large drive wheels in the rear, and had a bed that was about four feet wide, three feet high, and probably about 15 feet long. It was pulled by a team of two horses. The drive wheels drove three rotating "beaters" which were mounted in the rear. Two of the beaters were about 16 inches in diameter and were equipped with four inch long prongs. One of the beaters was mounted slightly above the top of the bed and slightly forward of the other similar pronged beater. The second pronged beater was mounted so that its prongs at the bottom were even with the bed bottom. The bottom of the bed was equipped with a conveyer consisting of cross bars driven by a chain on each side. These pulled the manure to the rear and into the beaters, where it was hit by the rotating beaters and pitched into the air and toward the rear where it hit the third beater, which was the last toward the rear at a level with the lowest pronged beaters. This third beater was equipped with slanted flat blades which pitched the manure to the side. The manure spreader was equipped with two control levers: one set the rate at which the conveyor pushed the manure toward the beaters and the other set the height of the last beater or spreader which controlled how far manure was pitched to the side.

On the front of the manure spreader was a metal seat on which the driver sat to drive the horses as the manure was spread.

Manure Spreader

The spreader was pulled alongside the open stable door for loading. The manure was pulled up with muscle power and a four-prong pitch fork and tossed out the door onto the spreader. It took a long time to load the spreader, especially if there were corn stalks mixed in with the manure which made it almost impossible to pull up. In a good day, 12 loads could be hauled out. In loading, care was taken not to load any soupy manure on the top of the load because the beaters would tend to pitch this forward onto the driver of the team.

The manure was hauled out in the spring and spread on the new wheat crop. During the winter it would collect in the stables up to three feet deep. My nephew, Daniel Schmidt, tells me that when he hauled manure, the manure was as much as six feet deep.

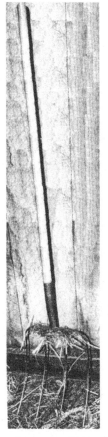

Four-Prong Pitchfork

We also had a straw pile, created when we threshed wheat. The cows fed on it in the winter, and this too generated manure around its base. After the stables were cleaned out, we then hauled out the straw pile manure. This wasn't quite as messy as the cow stable manure, neither was the horse manure.

We also raised chickens who generated manure. This manure was of a type different from cow manure or horse manure. It was generally light and gray and was picked up with a large scoop shovel and thrown onto the manure spreader through a small window in the rear of the hen house. This manure was extremely rich in nitrogen and the manure spreader was set on its lowest setting when the manure was spread. Even then, the manure was too rich for the wheat and the wheat would grow rank (tall) and often fall down before it could be cut. I sometimes wonder today why we didn't spread the chicken manure on the pasture instead of on the wheat.

There was another problem with chicken manure. A favorite food of the chickens when they were let out of the hen house was weed seed which they did not completely digest. So, wherever the manure was spread, weeds would grow about as well as the wheat.

Chicken manure had another attribute which was unpleasant and seldom mentioned. It often was dusty and one could not avoid breathing in the dust when loading it. There was something in this dust that left a sweet taste in the mouth, and one knew that this taste came from the chicken manure.

Today, of course, cow manure is picked up with tractor-mounted scoops and spread with tractor-pulled spreaders and there is hardly any horse manure. I don't know how chicken manure is disposed of today. It is probably bagged and sold as fertilizer, since the chickens are penned up and don't have a chance to get at weed seeds.

Needless to say, hauling manure was one farm job that tends to be forgotten with time because it is an unpleasant memory.

Field Naming

ALMOST EVERY FIELD on the farm had a name as did fields on other farms. We had a "Big Field," a "Clearing," a "Terrace Field," a "Hog Pasture," a "Stump Patch," two "Timothy Patches" (hay for the horses), a "Barn Lot," a "Field Behind The Barn," a "Hill Field," a "Three Corner Field," a "Flat," etc.

My uncle Frank had a "Lead Mine Ridge Field," a "Meisel Field," a "Round Bottom," a "Goose Neck," a "Ridge Field," an "Orchard Field," and more. It was a common practice for every farmer to name his fields. Of course, there were also "Hollers" (small valleys through which a creek ran) such as "Hootenanny Holler," "Renterghem's Holler," the "Wolken Holler," and "Carrender's Holler," although these "Hollers" often had different names depending upon the speaker's viewpoint. Sometimes, woods also had names such as the "Club Land." Of course there was the hog pasture in which was the "hog pasture spring" from which my grandmother got a bucket of water every day for years. There also was the "spring across the road" in the cow pasture.

Butchering Chickens

WE ALWAYS RAISED CHICKENS, both for eggs and for eating. In the late 1930s, before Dad built a weather-tight brooder house, we raised the baby chicks in an upstairs bedroom where we could put a heating stove to keep the place warm. The chicks would be delivered by the mailman in four-sectioned boxes with holes in them for air. We would get several hundred chicks. The floor of the upstairs bedroom was first lined with several layers of newspaper and a little straw was put on top of that. Then here came the chicks.

We had watering jars for the chicks to drink from and for the life of me I cannot remember what the chick feeders looked like. The waterers were quart mason jars onto which were screwed caps with a pan surrounding them. When a jar was inverted, the water would fill the pan but not overflow. To prevent certain chick diseases, such as coccidiosis, medicine of some type was added to the water.

One had to be careful with chicks because they were subject to all kinds of diseases and could not take temperature changes easily. When we first got electricity in 1941 or so, an electric brooder (pyramid shaped with four short legs at the corners) was substituted for the heating stove. The chicks created a lot of water vapor in the air and the windows would always be steamed up. Shortly after we got the electric brooder, the brooder house was built and the chick raising was moved there. There was a faux pas in building the brooder house, which also included a chimney for a wood stove after the chicks outgrew the brooder. Dad used fiber board for the ceiling, forgetting all about the large amount of water the chicks exhaled into the air. It wasn't long before the ceiling began to sag and pull loose.

Before the weather-tight brooder house, we had an intermediate chick house which was a shed-type affair on wooden runners. It was pulled out into a field and the chicks were transferred there when they reached around a pound in weight. The chicks could then feed on the grass surrounding the house. With the brooder house we had a fenced-in pen which the chick could access through a low door in the side of the brooder house. We had one disaster with the chick pen. A sister of my aunt Catherine gave us kids a small pup. One Sunday, when we were out visiting, the pup got in the pen and killed 63 chicks and piled them up. Only then did we discover that the pup was of a bird dog breed. He was gone to the hereafter before the evening was over.

Scale Used to Weigh Chickens

When the chickens got about two pounds in weight, they were moved to the chicken house, where they grew into hens and roosters. If we were raising eggs to be sold for eating, a rooster was an unnecessary drain on the economy so they were dispensable. When they got to be what we called broiler size we butchered them and sold the meat to groceries in Jefferson City which resold it. No government inspection then. On the day when Dad was going to town, after the milking, etc. was done, it was time to butcher the chickens. We would use a wire bent in a sort of shepherd's crook form with a narrow loop to catch the roosters by a leg and pull them out of the flock. The rooster selected was put on a scale to see if it was big enough. I found that if you laid a straw across a chicken's eye, it would lay on the scale and not move. The straw must have seemed like a log to it and impossible to dislodge. If you don't believe this, try it once.

We would take a rooster, pull back its wings and grasp them, along with both of the rooster's feet in one hand, and lay their neck across the chopping block, which was nothing more than a block of heating stove wood. One whack with the axe severed the head, which fell to the ground gasping for air and dying. The rest of the rooster would want to flop in its death throes but it was held tightly by the wings and feet over a five-gallon bucket to let the blood drain out through the neck arteries. This is not done today in processing plants and, as a result, the dressed chicken is bloody, especially the thigh and drumstick parts, and not very much to my liking.

After the chicken had quit its flopping, it was dunked into a five-gallon bucket of hot water to "scald" it. This loosened the feathers so they could be removed. Today this feather removal is done in a processing plant by rotating rubber knobs. Mom was insistent that we carefully grasp the feathers when pulling them out so that we also removed the fine hairs that occurred among the feathers, especially on the wings. Some people removed these hairs by singeing the chicken over a fire, but Mom would not allow this, claiming it ruined the chicken.

After the feathers were removed, the chicken was carefully disemboweled, rinsed several times in clean water, and then cut up into parts. This cutting up was not done with a shears, as is done today with the resulting misshapen parts and misplaced bone. Instead a "butcher" knife was used to precisely cut the chicken apart at the joints so that every thigh, drumstick, and wing looked exactly alike and was recognizable. We saved the legs, scalded them to remove the skin, and cooked them for soup along with the necks which also did not get sold. The breasts were removed and split in two. I don't believe we sold the backs, but I'm not sure. If we didn't sell them, we would have also cooked them in soup.

Sometimes the work was assigned to us as separate chores, such as Quentin cutting off the heads and Rod scalding and plucking, but quite often, each one rotated through the different tasks, except for disemboweling the chickens which Mom always did. The chicken parts were packed in cold well water and Dad headed to town with them along with roasting ears from a corn field if they were ready for eating. I can remember Dad getting 27¢ a dozen for roasting ears from the grocer. I don't remember any of the prices the chickens brought. We usually sold to Clyde Popp who ran a grocery store on Clark Avenue where the expressway goes through today or to the Kroger store either on Clark Avenue or on McCarty Street.

We butchered chickens until all the roosters were gone. We of course would butcher a couple when we had Sunday company. When the hens quit laying, they too met the butcher's block and went the way of the roosters, although at an inferior price. When they were gone, it was time for a new batch of chicks the following spring.

For a few years, we got "sexed" chickens, which meant that the male chicks were already sorted out and discarded. These chicks were intended to produce eggs for hatching which brought a premium of up to 10¢ a dozen over eating eggs. The sorting was reportedly done by Filipinos or Japanese who could tell the difference between a male and female chick. However, I never saw a Filipino or Japanese at the time and I believe this was pure fiction. A few roosters were included to fertilize the eggs. One rooster could "take care" of many hens. The chickens bought to produce hatching eggs were usually Leghorns. We bought, in different years, Rhode Island Reds and Plymouth Rocks which were meatier.

Chicken butchering was not as unpleasant as hauling manure, but it was also a task that was not remembered fondly.

Ole Barney

OLD BARNEY (he was young once) was a brownish black horse that stood about 17 hands (68 inches) tall. He was born in 1931 to a mare called Babe who belonged to my Mertens grandparents. Dad got both horses when my Mertens grandfather died in 1933.

If horses went to college, Barney would have graduated Magna Cum Laude plus. He was the smartest horse I ever knew. I don't know when he became smart, but he was that way for as long as I could remember. When he wanted out of the stable, he would just put his rump against the door and shove until the latch broke and out he would go. We tried to solve that by driving the door full of eight penny nails sticking through to the stable side. After a while, Barney decided that he would back up against the nails and move his rump sideways, bending the nails over. Then he just pushed against the bent over nails, broke the latch and out he would go. We even had our barn lot gates full of nails extending into the barn lot. This stopped him there because he would use his shoulders to push against the gate, and they must have been more tender than his rear end.

When it came time to get him out of the stable for real work, he had to be bridled first. If he was let loose without a bridle, just try to catch him or get him in the barn again! When you approached him with the bridle in the stable he would raise his head as high as he could. You could get the bit in his mouth but not the top of the bridle over his head. I would have to stand on the manger to bridle him. My brother Al would sometimes put a rope around his neck and pull it under a manger two-by-four and when Barney would lower his head a little, take up the slack until Barney's head was low enough to bridle him. This was later and I was never smart enough to try this.

Once the bridle was on his head and you led him out of the stable, he would drag a hind leg and groan like he was in pain. This never worked, but he kept doing it. At different times we had two cars that wouldn't start in the wintertime. For some reason, Dad seemed to always park the car in the garage then. That might have been because neither car had a heater and keeping them in the garage would have made the car interior warmer than if it had been outside. Cranking the cars by hand was impossible. In fact, we didn't have a crank for one of them. This meant putting the harness on ole Barney to pull the car out of the garage and up the driveway hill. After going through the bridle routine, and the dragging leg, came the job of putting the harness on him. He would be led to one door at the end of the barn hall where the harness was hung. Putting the collar on him was easy. The rest was not. The horse was tall. The top of his withers was at my eye level as an adult and much higher when I was a kid. The concrete foundation at the end of the hall was about three feet above the ground so one would push old Barney until his side was near the foundation. Then the harness would be lifted off the peg, a heavy job (it weighed 70 pounds), dragged to the end of the hall and, from there, thrown over Barney's back, or one hoped so. Most of the time Barney would sidestep at just the right moment so that the kid and the harness went plummeting to the ground. Then it was drag the harness back up the three feet and into the hall, go outside and kick Barney in the belly to move him over to the foundation again and try again. Barney would get tired of this and finally stand where he belonged and we would get the harness on. Another remedy was to use two kids, one to kick Barney to keep him near the foundation and the other to put the harness on.

1932 Model B Ford Like Ours

Then it was lead Barney to the car shed (with sometimes a repeat of the leg dragging and groaning) and hook him to the back bumper of the car with a single tree and chain so he could pull the car out of the shed. Unfortunately, we did not have a good log chain on the place, so we used old worn-out tire chains to hook onto the car bumper, which was a separate thing then. Well, Barney recognized that we didn't have a log chain and, when it came time for him to pull, he would suddenly lunge forward, the car would stand still, and the tire chain would break and Barney would rest. We got smart, and just as Barney would start to lunge, we would yank back on the bit and make him start gradually. The car would be pulled up the driveway and onto the road. We would unhook the chain from the back bumper, take Barney around to the front and hook him to the front bumper. Repeat of the lunge and yank back on the reins and the car would be going forward. Dad would have the car in low gear (so the engine would turn at a maximum rate compared to wheel revolutions) and would "pop" the clutch. Sometimes the engine would start right away and sometimes Barney had to keep pulling. However, one thing Barney knew. When the engine started, his job was done and he would stop dead in his tracks. Dad would have to quickly apply the brakes to keep from running into him. I think I would have let it hit him once or twice so he would learn a lesson.

At various times we worked Barney with other horses and Barney quickly found out the weakness of each of them. If the other horse had a tendency to balk (refusal to pull) Barney would exploit this in his own unique way. On the command, "Giddap", he would lunge forward pulling the other horse at the end of the double tree backward into the load. The other horse would assume the load was too much and refuse to pull. Or if the other horse was excitable, it would then try to pull and Barney would back up and you would have the horses seesawing back and forth and the load going nowhere. This often happened when pulling a load of hay. A convenient pitch fork convinced Barney to stop those antics.

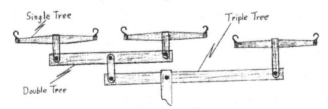

Triple Tree Arrangement for Three Horses

Barney was smart in other ways too. When we cut wheat or oats with a binder, three horses were required. Often the two other horses would not get along and we would have to put Barney in the middle. This would put Barney on the end of the double tree that was just ahead of the triple tree. A bit of explanation is required here. Two horses were hooked to the ends of the double tree which had a hole in its center. The double tree was attached by this hole to one end of the triple tree and the third horse was hooked to the other end of the triple tree. The triple tree lever arm for the single horse was twice as long as the double tree side so all horses pulled equally. However, if the center horse let back, that end of the double tree would rest against the triple tree and the two outside horses would pull the whole load. This was one of Barney's favorite tricks. He would ease back until his double tree end hit the triple tree and would walk along keeping his tugs taut, making it look like he was pulling. Only if one looked down and saw the double tree touching the triple tree would one recognize that he was loafing. To this end we carried a load of small rocks in the binder tool box and would get one out and pelt Barney's rear end with one when he slacked off. He did this often enough that the triple tree had a groove in it where the double tree hit.

If you got tired of rock throwing and yelling at

Barney and put him at the other end of the double tree near the standing grain side, he would eat the grain as he walked along. To prevent this, a muzzle made of one inch mesh chicken wire was placed over the horse's nose to hold his jaws nearly closed. Barney could outwit this by ducking his head straight up and down pushing the grain heads between his lips. His muzzle had to have screen wire over the chicken wire.

I digress here a moment to tell about one of the tools we used that is seen only in museums today. That was a draw knife. One is pictured below. The draw knife was used to shape wood for single or double trees, wooden wagon wheel spokes, wagon bolsters, etc. It was held in both hands and the wood was trimmed by drawing the knife toward you, hence the name.

Draw Knife

I have already mentioned the problem with plowing. If Barney was walking on the unplowed ground, he would ease over against the horse in the furrow so that a full width of the plow would not be used, making the plow easier to pull. If you put him in the furrow he would also ease over toward the plowed ground so you had to be on guard either way. Also, if you hit a stump, Barney would wait until you had the plow almost loose and backed out and he would then lunge forward and stick the plow into or under the stump again.

Barney had a keen ear. When cutting hay with the mower, which had a reciprocating sickle bar, the mower produced distinctive sounds. Some hay, especially that with certain grasses such as wire grass, was extremely hard to cut and would tend to bunch up in front of the mower bar. This changed the sound of the mower and Barney was quick to take advantage. He would immediately slow down and the sickle bar would clog up with the grass. To get going again, the mower was stopped, giving Barney a rest of course, put out of gear (to avoid having fingers cut off) and the sickle bar would have to be kicked one way or another to loosen the bar so the grass could be removed by hand from in between the mower guards. This took some time which is just what

Barney wanted.

If we were working with machinery out in a far field such as the big field at dinnertime (lunch to city folks) we would unhook the horses and ride them back to the house and barn where we would both eat. Barney resented a rider on his back. To give him credit he never bucked. Probably because he never learned how or he would have done it. But he surely resented that rider. We would be going through the woods toward home when Barney would suddenly change direction to pass under a low tree limb to try to unseat the rider. If this didn't work, he would move further to the side and try to rub off the rider against a tree trunk. A smart rider soon became aware of Barney's tricks and countered them, at least to the extent of raising his leg out of the way of the tree trunk. But that wasn't the end of it. When we got to the barn lot, we would head the horses to the water trough to water them. This was another opportunity for Barney. He would stiffen his rear end raising it as high as possible and lower his front end as much as possible trying to get the rider to slide forward into the water trough.

Barney had yet another trick. We would not take the harness off the horses when we put them in the stable at dinner time and this gave Barney another opportunity. Harnesses had what we called flank straps which came around the sides of the horse's rear end and fastened with a snap to a strap that went forward to the neck yoke which allowed the horse to push a load backward. Well, Barney would carefully raise one of his hind legs and hook it over one of the flank straps and stand there on three legs with the weight of his one leg pulling down on the flank strap. To straighten this mess out, his leg would have to be raised, no easy task when he resisted, so that the flank strap could be unsnapped and re-snapped where it belonged. Barney never did this more than once at a time because he knew he would get some swift kicks in the belly if he did. He didn't just do this in the stable. You could have him standing at a threshing machine and be unloading wheat and discover, when you were ready to drive away, that he was "three legged".

We sometime used him to plow in the garden between sweet corn rows with a double shovel plow. This was an adventure. Barney could walk what I would call sideways, that is, his hind end would not track his front end. This enabled him to step on the corn plants with his hind legs while going straight between the rows with his front end. He also loved doing this when he was part of a team used with a cultivator to plow corn. Aggravating as hell.

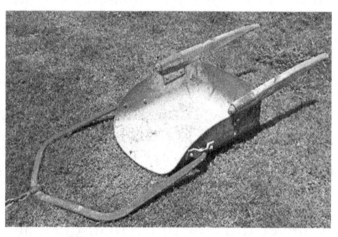

Horse-Drawn Dirt Scoop

When we dug a basement for the house remodeling, we removed the top dirt with a horse-drawn scoop. One is shown below in the dumped position. One or two horses were hooked to the front of the scoop and the operator used the two handles attached to the sides of the scoop. To scoop up dirt the operator would lift the handles and drive the horses forward filling the scoop with dirt. When the scoop was full the operator would bear down on the handles lifting the front out of the dirt and drive the load to the dump spot. There he would lift the handles to dig the front into the dirt and allow the handles to go fully forward, dumping the dirt.

The last two feet of the basement consisted of foot thick soft limestone rocks. We would wrap a chain (by that time we had a log chain) around a large rock and hook Barney to it and he would drag it out behind the henhouse. We broke up most of the rocks and buried them in the sidewalks we poured on the place. The sidewalks were 18 inches deep and never "heaved" from frost.

Barney had a tough hide. He could stand still with 20 horseflies (ten times bigger than a large house fly) sucking blood out of his hide. The bite of one of those flies was many times worse than a hypodermic needle jab. However, bot flies would drive him up the wall. Bot flies would bite the horse under the neck and this must have been a sensitive spot.

There was another problem with Barney. On the farm, horses wore steel shoes on their hooves. And, yes, the blacksmith didn't do it, we put the shoes on the horses ourselves. After the hoof was trimmed with a horseshoe knife, the hoof was leveled exactly with a rasp, and then the steel shoes were nailed on with horseshoe nails. Instead of exactly leveling the hoof, a professional horseshoer (farrier is the fancy name) would heat the iron red hot and place it on the hoof to burn in an exact fit. We didn't do it this way.

Typical Horseshoe Knife

Horseshoe nails had a bevel on one side of the point so, as they were driven into the hoof, they bent in a curve and came out the side where they were clinched over and filed down to hold the shoe on. Well, we didn't have any special apparatus to hold up the horse's leg when we were doing this and had to hold the horse's leg between our knees. We also did not have a leather apron like that worn by professional farriers. This was no major problem until it came to nailing on the shoe. As the nail exited the side of the hoof, there was a one-inch length of pointy nail pointing right at the horseshoer's knees. Barney loved to pull down on his leg at just such moments. One soon learned to quickly bend the nail upward with the hammer claws to prevent a painful wound.

Shoeing Pretense, but How It Was Done

I will insert something here that I had forgotten until I was reminded by my brother Clarence. Barney liked to step on human feet. He often did this, especially when you tried to bridle him in the stable. You soon learned that trying to push him off was counter-productive. He would only put more of his weight upon your foot. The only solution was to hit or kick him in the belly to get him to move. His step could be quite painful, especially if you were barefoot.

Horseshoe Nails

Now, I've got to say that, despite his tricks, Barney was a good work horse and could pull as much as two other horses and did so sometimes when the other horse of the team balked. Barney lived to be 21 years old and went as mink feed at that age.

I was out of college by then and working in Philadelphia where my company forced me, along with many others, to take a speech course. I won first prize at the end of the course for my speech which was a funeral sermon (or eulogy) for old Barney. May he rest in peace!

Putting Up Hay

WHEN I WAS A KID, putting up hay was done quite differently than it is today. There were two kinds of hay, regular and stubble. The regular hay had been sown the year before. Stubble hay was hay that was sown on wheat or oats in the spring and cut the same summer as the grain was harvested. It therefore had the wheat or oat stubble in it and hence the name. I guess to be fully complete, I should say that there were lespedeza hay, timothy hay, red top, clover, alfalfa, and fescue. The timothy hay was reserved for the horses (cows wouldn't eat it) and had a straight stalk with a long fuzzy head at the top. We grew it on the top part of the hill behind the barn and near the top of the hill east of the barn. Both patches were rocky and good for little else. By the way, the east patch was near an outcropping of flint and we always speculated that Indians had used the flint for arrow heads. This was because there were many apparently half-finished arrow heads there.

Broadcast Seeder

Hay seed was always sown in February when the ground was frozen. It was sown by hand with a "broadcast" seeder. This consisted of a bag, held by a shoulder strap, which contained the seed and connected to about a three-foot long metal tube that was crisscrossed with four wires to spread the seed. The flow of seed was adjustable where the bag connected to the tube. The operator tied a white string to the fence at the start point and walked toward a point on the opposite fence, swinging the tube and spreading the seed as he went. At the end of his trip he tied a white rag on the fence where he started from and went back across the field. The flow of seed was stopped by the simple process of pointing the tube skyward.

Lespedeza was leafy hay and was quite popular when I was a kid. However, the nutrients it required finally were exhausted and it didn't grow very well. Alfalfa took a lot of water and was not grown much except in bottom land. Red top and fescue are similar, being grasses with wide-spreading heads of grain at the top of a stem. The red top grain was reddish and thus the name. Clover was also leafy hay, but it had relatively large roundish seed heads about an inch in diameter. Before they dried, parts of the clover seed heads could be pulled out and the bottom ends sucked on for a little sweet nectar. Clover was very dusty hay and we didn't use it much. Once in a while it was raised for seed and was run through a threshing machine. Anyone who worked near the machine turned black with the dust. There also always was an assortment of wild grasses and weeds that grew along with the desired hay.

Putting up hay began with cutting it down with a horse-drawn mower. The mower had two drive wheels with small cleats on the rims. Through a gearing mechanism, they drove a pitman back and forth at the front of the mower, which was connected to a sickle perpendicular to the side of the mower. The sickle contained side-by-side triangular blades which traveled back and forth between and above pointy guards, each of which contained a serrated blade against which the sickle cut the hay.

A mower was heavy and the horses' necks carried the weight through the tongue. I always thought this was a poor balance arrangement but realize now that the weight served to give the relatively small drive wheels traction on the cut hay. Besides, the weight of the driver on the seat in the rear counterbalanced some of the weight on the tongue. The mower always traveled on the hay cut the previous round. The metal bar holding the sickle and the guards was called just that, the bar. It was about six feet long and had a wood board at the end which pulled the cut hay a little way away from the uncut hay. This was necessary to prevent cut hay from clogging up the mower blades on the next round.

Mowing Hay

I mentioned before the problem with Barney recognizing the sound of the mower when the cutting got hard and slowing down to clog the mower, so no more need be said on that point. When cutting hay there was always the possibility of cutting off a leg of a rabbit or cutting a snake into parts, but this didn't happen too often.

After the hay was cut, it had to be allowed to dry or it would mold in the barn and be worthless. This usually took a day or so depending on the weather. Hay that got rained on lost much of its value. After the hay was dry, it was raked up with a dump rake. This was an apparatus with narrow but high wheels (about six feet in diameter) spaced about 12 feet apart. Between the wheels was a set of curved tines that dragged along the ground at the rear of the rake and collected the hay ahead of them. The tines were about four inches apart and formed into half-circles about three feet in diameter. When the area in front of the tines was full of hay, the driver, who sat on a seat in the middle of the rake, kicked down a pedal. This engaged a gear on each wheel, causing the tines to rotate upward and dump the hay. The rake was mechanized such that it automatically returned the tines to the ground as soon as the hay was dumped. If someone was free, he would pile this 12-foot length of hay into one pile for loading on a wagon. Dad was never too good about fixing machinery and the seat on the hay rake would wobble from side to side, making it difficult for a kid to reach the dumping pedal. Also, a kid could easily fall off the seat and my brother Albert tells a harrowing tale of one time when this happened to him.

After the hay was raked, the hauling in began. This required at least two people, one to pitch the hay on the wagon and the other to "stomp" or pack it down. This stomping was necessary.

Without it, the wagon would hold very little hay. We went barefoot in the summer and the soles of our feet were toughened so ordinarily stomping hay was no problem. However, the toughness did not apply to the arches and sides of our feet which remained tender. The hay often had what we called dewberry vines and bull nettles that had a tendency to puncture the tender parts of the feet. Stomping hay was no picnic. It took quite a while to load a wagon of hay. The load when finished was about ten feet wide, ten feet high and 20 feet long, so a load contained a lot of hay.

Cousin Anstine Veit Showing Height of Hay Load, Manure Spreader and Straw Pile in Background

The last time I hauled hay before going away to college, my cousin Anstine Veit helped me load it and my brother Al did the stomping. The wagon we used had two rubber tires in the front and two steel wheels in the back, the only hybrid wagon in Osage Bend. All four wheels had tapered sleeve bearings which used black axle grease. The wheels were held onto this tapered bearing (on the end of the wooden axle) by square nuts, about three inches across the flats. See picture below.

Typical Steel Wagon Wheels

We had hauled in 50 loads that year, which almost filled the barn to the top. We had two more loads to go when my brothers Rod and Clarence came out from their jobs in Jefferson City and volunteered to get the last two loads while I started the milking. What a mistake! They tried to put the two loads on one and while driving the load to the barn managed to turn it over in the field across the road. The two loads of hay remained in the field and rotted, and the beautiful white hay frame I had just built that spring got broken. It was a while before I forgave them.

One year we had a lot of hay and we hired the Sommer boys, Max and Hermann, to bale hay for us. They had a McCormick Deering "M" tractor (big) and a side pick-up baler. They hired Henry Rackers to backwire on the baler. In baling, as the hay is compressed in a rectangular cylinder, a wooden block is dropped every so often to separate the hay into bales. The block has four slots, two on the rear and two on the front. Wire is fed through the front two slots on the rear block in the baler and back through the rear two slots on the front block. This allows the block to come free when the bale is ejected. The wiring is done while the baler is moving and the hay is moving in the cylinder. Feeding the wire back through is done by the backwirer as is the block dropping. The backwirer sat behind the hay pickup mechanism and got all the dust from the hay. It was the job of the tier on the other side of the baler to feed the wire through the first block and tie the wire when it was fed back to him. He tightened and wrapped the wire while the baler was doing its compression stroke so the wire was taut. While this crew was baling, I was cutting and raking.

When they stopped for a smoke break, they discovered that no one had a dry match or a lighter although they had cigarettes. I suggested that they drip a little gasoline from the tractor tank on a cigarette, remove a wire from a spark plug, and while holding the gasoline-soaked tip between the wire and the spark plug, crank the tractor. It worked like a charm! At the first spark, the end of the cigarette burst into flame and they had their light. I heard about my "smarts" from Max every time I saw him after that. I didn't participate in the smoke break because I had not yet begun to smoke and also could not have come up with the money to buy any cigarettes.

I forgot to mention that there were also two other hay-making machines which we did not have nor did we use. One was a hay loader which was pulled behind the wagon and which brought the hay up onto the wagon with a chain-driven and rotating tine conveyor system. This was not so hot because the hay still had to be moved from the back of the wagon to the front. My uncle Frank had one, but seldom used it. The other machine was called a hay tedder. It was a horse-drawn device that is difficult to describe. As it was pulled along, it picked up the hay with rotating prongs and sort of turned it over. It was used if the hay was exceedingly thick so that the cut hay on the bottom would dry or after rain so the hay would dry. My uncle Frank also had one of these.

In later years after I had left home, Dad got a tractor and had a tractor-mounted mower. He also had a side-delivery rake that put the hay into windrows. This was followed by a pick-up baler which picked the hay from the windrows and compressed it into bales that were tied with twine.

The Terrace Field

WHEN WE MOVED ONTO THE PLACE, the field up the road from the house had mostly grown up in brush and had ditches as deep as a horse. My dad and mom decided to rescue the field and make use of it. We cut off the brush and piled it in the ditches to fill them up. To prevent them from washing out again the field was terraced. This is where I learned about laying out terraces.

Dad got a transit and marking pole from the conservation agent and we set to work. The transit, which could be accurately leveled, sat on a tripod. It contained a telescope that was the thing being leveled. The transit was set up near where a terrace was to begin and leveled. I held the marking pole at the terrace starting point and moved a guide on it until it could be seen at the cross hairs in the transit. I drove a small stake in the ground at that point. I then raised the guide by a half-inch and paced off 50 feet. Dad then waved me uphill or downhill until the guide again fell on the cross hairs. Here I again drove in a stake at the base of the leveling pole. I moved the guide up another half-inch and repeated the process. In this way we marked out the location of a terrace that would have a drop of one inch to 100 feet. Since the longest terrace was 1000 feet long and ran around a hill, the transit had to be moved several times, each time starting out at the last point. In this way we marked out three or four terraces in the field.

Dad then got Alvin Lehman, who had a tractor-drawn grader, to follow the stakes and grade up terraces on the field. The terraces were there at least 20 years before they were redone. The field is still known as the "Terrace Field."

I told the above as though I was the one who moved the leveling pole and drove the stakes. In fact, I no longer remember whether I did one of the jobs or both, but I'm positive I did one of them.

Planting Corn

SOME FARMERS PLANTED THEIR CORNFIELDS with hills of corn evenly spaced in both directions, called "check-rowing." A neatly checked field of corn allowed cultivation in both directions for improved weed control, and the symmetry of it was a delight to behold. Check-rowing was accomplished by stretching a special wire along the intended row. The wire had nodes, like knots, every 42 inches, the same spacing as the corn rows. The corn planter was equipped with a Y-shaped trigger through which the wire was fed. Whenever the trigger encountered one of the nodes in the wire it would be pulled backward, causing the seed to drop at that point. After the drop, the node would ride out over the trigger, and a spring would return the trigger to its forward position, ready for the next drop. To be successful, one needed to start with a straight row, then had to reposition the trip wire with care, maintaining the same amount of tension on one side of the field as on the other.

We checked corn only once to my knowledge. That was after Dad replaced his old corn planter with a newer one that came with the check wire. Checking corn was a pain and I don't believe we even plowed the corn crossways that time.

One of the "joys" of growing corn was plowing it. We had two types of corn cultivators. One of these was called a walking cultivator. The operator walked behind the cultivator, guiding four plow "shovels" with a pair of wooden handles. He had to walk beside the row of corn but keep the plows aligned one on each side of the row. In other words, he worked sideways. Unless of course the corn was small and then he could have straddled the row, but that would have meant walking with his feet always apart sideways, so he walked down between the rows. The "shovels" were equipped with spring trips so they could trip backward if they hit a solid object like a stump or a rock. The "shovel" had to be lifted up to allow it to spring back forward. The lines to the horses were tied together behind the operator's back and he guided the horses by twisting his torso. This wasn't too bad with a team of horses that would walk between the rows without much guidance. But remember, we had old Barney and that made things difficult.

Plowing Corn with a Riding Cultivator

The other type of cultivator was a riding cultivator. Here the operator sat on a metal seat (by the way, such seats got exceedingly hot if exposed to the sun for any length of time) and guided the wheels with his feet. This sounds easier but wasn't. Remember old Barney. Also, if the wheels got too far from straight alignment, the operator lost his mechanical advantage and it became quite difficult to control them. The "shovels' on this cultivator could be replaced with rotating disks which were used to "lay by" the corn, that is throw a ridge of dirt toward the row and on top of the higher roots. This "laying by" was the last cultivation the corn got.

Of course there was the "joy" of cutting the corn and shocking it or picking the ears off by hand. We usually needed the corn fodder so we cut it and put it in shocks.

Corn Shocks

In the earliest years we raised corn on "new ground" which was rich in nutrients. In later years, after Dad got the bottom land from his dad, we raised corn only in the bottom. Here we had to contend with the Union Electric Bagnell Dam which caused the bottom land to flood seven years out of the first eight we had it.

The corn cutting was done with a corn knife,

which today might be called a machete. When a shock was to be made, four stalks, two each from adjacent rows, were bent and tied together near the top. This formed the framework against which the first stalks were leaned. My uncle Frank had a corn binder which would cut the corn and tie it up in bundles. We never used it.

Milking

WHEN WE LIVED UP THE ROAD, we milked cows for their cream, which we made into butter and perhaps sold. If we sold it, we would have sold it to Emil Hirschman up at Osage Bluff. The skim milk would have gone to feed a pig or two. I remember a butter churn in the front room that I supposedly broke, so I'm sure about the butter. I can't remember exactly, but we must have had about 10 cows.

When we moved down the road, we continued milking for cream. The cream separator was kept in the smoke house and I can remember it being used there. I didn't have to do it, but I remember that it was a dog to wash. There were about 20 to 30 cone-shaped discs that formed the heart of the centrifuge that separated the cream. Then also, there were the big bowl and housing that surrounded the centrifuge discs. Sometime around 1940, a neighbor began to haul bulk milk to Linn, Missouri to a creamery there and we began to sell bulk milk.

We milked 10 to 12 cows morning and evening and kept the bulk milk in the well house in a concrete vat to keep it cool. The bulk milk was picked up once every two days. We had to carry our milk up to the road where it was picked it up. The milk was not refrigerated while it stood there, nor was the truck, so, not infrequently, we got back a can of sour milk. Mom put the curds of this onto a tea towel which she then tied up and hung on the clothes line to drain. This we ate as cottage cheese with cinnamon and sugar. I absolutely abhorred it.

We had a motley assortment of cows, some Jerseys, a Guernsey or two, but mostly a mixed Holstein breed. The Jerseys gave the richest milk (most cream) and the Holsteins gave the most milk. They had a variety of teat sizes, the Jersey's were very small and short and the Holstein's very big and long. I had short fingers but a broad hand so none of them fit. My fingers were right for the

Jerseys but my hand was too wide and my hand was okay for the Holsteins but my fingers were too short. Milking was always a chore for me and I disliked it enormously.

One summer I worked for Uncle Rudolph and he had 10 milking goats which I had to milk. The goats had two teats compared to the cow's four, but their teats were very long and big around. Other than Aunt Josephine's complaints about my slowness in milking cows, goat milking was what I hated the most at Uncle Rudolph's.

We used one-legged stools and two and one-half gallon, tin-plated milk buckets while milking the cows. When the bucket got full we carried it up to the well house where we emptied it into a strainer set into the top of the ten-gallon can. The strainer had a removable circular cotton pad which provided the straining. Straining was needed because we did not wash the cow's udders (we called them bags) before milking and dirt on their udders would wind up in the milk. After the milking was completed, we would remove the strainer and throw the pad out of the well house where the numerous cats would attack it with gusto. Of course, they paid for it, because they swallowed the cotton of which the pad was made and had trouble with later bowel movements. The lid was placed on the 10-gallon can and the can set in the cooling vat.

On the morning the milk was picked up, we had to make sure that the milking was done before the truck came by, and I think this may have been part of our sour milk problems. If we did not get through with the milking early enough, the latest milk would not have had time to cool down before we carried it up to the road.

Ten-Gallon Milk Can

This carrying of the milk up to the road was a quite a task. Ten gallons of milk by itself weighs

80 pounds, and adding 10 or more pounds for the metal can, the total weight of a can of milk came to 90 or more pounds. This was quite a load for a kid to handle, especially because the can was so awkward to carry. If you grabbed it by one handle, you had to hold it up instead of letting it hang from your hand because the can was too tall. If you held it by both handles, you had to hold it out in front of you so it would not hit your legs as you walked. Luckily, there often was another kid to help carry it up to the road, but this also had its problems. The shortest kid had to hold his side up high enough to keep the can from hitting the taller kid in the side of his leg or ankle. Woe to the short kid who let his side down. It would have been nice to have a cart to haul it on. Oh well, we got the cans up there.

Cows had names. We had a Kicky Micky, a Blackie, a Spot, etc. We had one Jersey which hated anything in skirts. This traced back to when she had a calf one time and one of my sisters saw it and squealed. She would chase any skirt after that. It should be obvious where Kicky Micky got her name.

In the summertime we milked the cows outside

in the barn lot. I was milking one time when a red fox came running down the driveway and paused by the barn lot fence and just stared at me. He stayed there for many minutes until he heard the hounds that were chasing him get too close. Then he just trotted away.

We had some cows that would push through a barbed wire fence or just jump over it. We took care of this by putting a yoke with top and bottom extensions around their necks. This kept them from pushing through a fence. To combat the fence jumpers, we put a chain around their necks with a large hook attached which would catch on the fence when they jumped it.

When a cow came into heat it was obvious and we drove the cow up to Uncle George's to be serviced by his bull. Amazingly, he had one bull which could service a cow 10 or more times in 10 minutes. In later years, Dad got a bull of his own.

Hog Butchering

EVERY YEAR, late in the fall, we butchered six to eight 200 pound hogs for our own use. The day before the butchering, a platform about four feet wide was built upon two saw horses. A large wooden barrel was nailed by its top edge to one end of the platform. Because of its height, the barrel would rest on a slant. Near the bottom of the barrel on one side there was a hole that accommodated a two-inch diameter pipe with stuffing around it to prevent leaks. The pipe was about 12 feet long and capped on the end not in the barrel. This capped end was placed on a rock or two so the pipe was approximately level, but with the capped end just a little higher than the barrel end. Wood for a fire was placed under the pipe near the rock. The barrel was filled with water and we were set for the butchering the next day.

Before any chores were started the next day, the fire was lit under the pipe. By the time the chores were done and breakfast eaten, the water in the barrel was at about the right temperature. When the water in the pipe over the fire heated to the boiling point it would suddenly expand into steam and force the water in the pipe into the barrel. Cooler water would then rush into the pipe and the cycle was ready to repeat. This was the way the water in the wooden barrel was heated.

Setup for Scalding Hogs

I liked the sound of the water heating because it had a distinctive snapping sound when the water was forced into the barrel. This technique was the basis for a toy "motor" boat that my friend, Albert Renterghem, had. It had a small tin "boiler" in the front under which sat a candle. A small tube extended from the "boiler" to the rear of the boat under the water line. When the tank was filled with water and the candle lit, the thing would go "putt-putting" along in the water.

With the water hot, we were ready to start butchering. Uncle George often helped us, and when he did, he always shot the hogs. We used a single-shot .22 caliber rifle with long rifle shells. The hog had to be shot head on in the center of the forehead, so that none of the meat was ruined by the bullet. When Uncle George was not around, I got the task of shooting the hogs. A well-shot hog dropped immediately. Two people rushed in and turned the hog upside down and one of them stabbed the hog through the neck into the heart to bleed it. The blood would come gushing out. Some people saved the blood for blood sausage, but we never did.

Once the hog was bled, it was carried to the platform and two men (or one man and a big boy,) one on each side of the hog, dipped the hog in the hot water in the barrel. This loosened the hair. The hog had to be turned around to dip both ends. This wasn't too easy because the hogs weighed 200 pounds. Once it was properly dipped, the hog was attacked with knifes held perpendicular to the hide to scrape off the hair which, because of the scalding, would come out of its follicles.

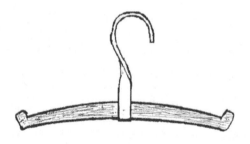

Wooden Gambrel with Iron Hanging Hook

After the hair was removed from the hog, the back of the hind legs just above the ankle was slit and the end of a wooden gambrel was inserted under the leg tendon in each leg. The hog was then ready to hang up to complete the butchering. The hog was carried into the well house and the gambrel placed over an iron hook suspended from a stringer (ceiling crosspiece tying the well house together.) While one person held a washtub to catch the entrails, another slit the hog's belly from the rear end to the chest. The large intestines were discarded, but the small one was saved to be used as casing for sausage. The gutted hog was allowed to cool while another hog bit the dust.

The jowls (cheeks) of the hog were cut off and saved to be fried as bacon. The head was cut off and the tongue cut out. The brains were removed to be fried. These wouldn't keep with no refrigeration and we ate them the same day. My mother and I were about the only ones who cared for the brains. The rest of the head, including the ears but not the eyes, went into a large iron kettle to be cooked. The lungs, heart, sweetbreads, stomach, and kidneys went into the kettle too, along with the pig's tail. The liver was saved to be eaten separately. This was one of my least favorite meats. The tenderloins were taken out and went into sausage. In later years after we got electricity, we had a deep freeze (no refrigerator) and we froze some of the tenderloins. They were a delicacy. Many people kept the tenderloin with the backbone and sawed it up as pork chops. We never did. Any excess fat was removed and set aside to be ground up and rendered into lard.

At this point, an axe was used to cut the ribs

along the backbone and the backbone was removed. Mom cut the vertebra apart and canned the pieces to use in backbone soup. The shoulders were cut off and trimmed and put aside to be cured for later use. Much of the front legs were cut off the shoulders and were set aside to be canned as pig's feet. The ribs were removed from each side. The legs were cut off the hams and the hams were trimmed and set aside to be cured and the hind legs also went into the pig's feet.

Sausage Stuffer Minus Nozzle

The scraps from trimming the shoulders, hams, and other parts of the hog were ground in a sausage grinder to make sausage. Some people actually cut up shoulders and made them into sausage. We didn't, and consequently we didn't have much sausage. Mom canned most of the sausage, but some was hung on a string in the smoke house. The small intestines served as the casing for the sausage. They were turned inside out and the inner lining was scraped off with a dull knife. They were then washed many times and then, one at a time, slipped over the nozzle of the sausage press. The sausage press held about a gallon and a half of ground sausage. When the crank was turned a screw pressed a plate down on the sausage and squeezed it out the nozzle at the bottom and into the sausage casing.

The miscellaneous pieces such as the head were cooked in the iron kettle until the meat fell off the bone. While it was cooking, it was stirred occasionally with a wooden paddle. When the meat was done, the bones were fished out and the meat was run through the sausage grinder. It was packed in pint jars and canned. We called it "liver" sausage, but it had no liver in it. Instead, it was a close relative to head cheese. The pig's tail rarely made it into the liver sausage. It was the most delicious part of the hog and got fished out of the kettle and eaten right there.

The next day was cleanup day. The pig's feet were dipped in hot water to loosen the toe nails which were removed. The legs were sawed up into short lengths and canned without any pickling. I never could stand pickled pig's feet. Dad would chop the ribs up into three-inch lengths with an axe and these were canned. Some of the jowls and bacon were sliced and fried and then packed in lard in 10-gallon crocks. This was called "fried-down bacon" and was the best bacon.

It was also the day for rendering lard. The fat was ground up in the sausage grinder and then cooked in the same iron kettle used for cooking the parts that went into the liver sausage. When the fat was done cooking, it was placed in the sausage stuffer which was this time lined with a metal strainer. The cooked fat was compressed in the stuffer to force out all the lard. What was left in the stuffer was called "cracklins" and was good tasting but so "rich" that little could be eaten at a time.

The shoulders, hams, and bacon were packed in lots of salt in the meat box. The salt "cured" them and they would keep all year, even in hot weather.

After the hams and shoulders had cured, they usually were hung up instead of being left in the meat box. In the summertime we would occasionally go out to the smoke house and slice a piece off of a ham or shoulder and eat it right there without cooking it.

Woods

I ALREADY TOLD ABOUT THE WOODS across the road that we played in when we lived up the road. On our new place down the road, there were lots more woods. It was mostly scrub post oak with some hickory, walnut, black oak, and white oak mixed in. The really good trees were behind the "big field" in the "holler" behind it, and in the Wolken "holler." Some of these made good logs and were cut down and sawed into lumber for the new barn. Dad and Uncle Emil cut these but left one big hickory tree that leaned at a frightful angle. They didn't cut it because they figured it would split before they could cut all the way through it. Later, Dad and I risked it and sawed "like hell" with the crosscut to get it cut across before it split while we were felling it. We were successful and the trunk was sawed up into wagon tongues. I don't believe we used more than one or two of the tongues. Dad gave the rest away.

We pastured our cows in the woods across the road. There is normally not much pasture under trees that are allowed to grow close together and the cows would have starved if we had not cut a swath of brush and trees along the field fence across the road and a patch along part of the big field. Bringing the cows home for milking was a kid's task. Needless to say, the cows were never near home. They were usually around the big field when we went to get them. They had a regular path from the big field, by the spring and up the hill toward home. This path was a meandering thing going around brush and rocks and whatever else the cows wanted to avoid. The spring was an important part of the pasture. It was along the creek in the holler that started below the house and just across the road. Dad had built a concrete wall around the spring to hold water for the cows to drink. The spring never did flow heavily. It dried up after I left home and Dad built a pond across the road. In later years the spring began to flow again.

In the spring, wild onions grew like wildfire and were a favorite food for the cows when they were first put in the pasture in the springtime. The onion smell and taste permeated the milk which was unsaleable and virtually unusable for the first few days when the cows started in the pasture. Wild lily-like flowers grew in the gravel along the cow path in early spring. Later, other kinds of wild flowers also showed up and we sometimes picked a bouquet for Mom.

In the spring we hunted wild mushrooms in the woods. We only looked for and would only eat Morels and Red Mushrooms. Morels were hollow and quite a few were required to make a meal. The red ones were solid all the way through and only a couple would make a meal.

Morel Mushroom

Dad had an eye for mushrooms and could spot them from a moving car. It was simply amazing. One time we were going up the road along the Meisel tract (now part of the Braun farm) and Dad spotted some red ones in the woods. He picked them and found that they were not the regular red mushrooms, but what we later learned were called "Elephant Ears." Dad thought they were not good to eat, but took them along to Emil Hirschmann's. Emil identified them and said he would take them if Dad did not want them. Emil got them.

Mom couldn't find a mushroom if it bit her. In the 1960s Mom and Dad came down to Florissant to visit us one weekend and that Sunday morning I had found half a grocery bag full of Morels. Mom insisted that I take her back to where I found them so she could look for some more. I did and as we were walking, Mom almost stepped on two of them. I told her to stop and look around. It took her quite some time before she located the two. In another year, I took Dad to Babler State Park to look for mushrooms. I found a bunch of Morels and Dad found a bunch of what looked identical to Morels but were black. Again, neither he nor I would trust eating them and he gave them to someone there who said they were edible.

Striped Bark Scorpion

The woods across the road had limestone ledges and these were a favorite habitat for scorpions. You could turn over a rock there and find 20 to 30 of the creatures. A scorpion is poisonous and is to be avoided. It carries a stinger in its elongated tail. When it attacks, it coils up its tail and snaps the tail down, puncturing the skin and then walks along cutting a track into which it injects its poison. I don't believe the ones we had were fatal but they sure hurt like hell. My sister Catherine was stung by one on our front porch and screamed like she was dying from the pain. The cut was washed out with kerosene and that was that.

On the limestone ledges there was what we called a "wet weather" spring. After a rain, it would gush with about a one and a half inch diameter for about a day. Then it would quit. Springs weren't unusual in the area. I already told about the one that came up in our cistern. There were several that made their appearance in the terrace field.

Steel Wedges

The woods across the road were our source of fuel for the wood stoves and later for the furnace. The wood usually would be cut in the late fall or early winter after the sap had gone down, although we did cut some in late winter sometimes. We notched the trees with an axe and then cut them the rest of the way through with the crosscut saw to fell them. We generally cut the smaller trees and trimmed the limbs off and hauled the trees to where we would saw them up into firewood lengths. Occasionally we would cut down a larger tree that had to be split. This was done with steel wedges and a sledge hammer. The limbs we trimmed off were burned in brush piles. It was amazing how rapidly the wood burned once the pile was set afire.

Some neighbors left the brush piles unburned and these became havens for rabbits in the wintertime. When we went rabbit hunting, we stomped on these brush piles to bring out the rabbits so we could shoot them. We didn't hunt very often, but our Braun uncle and cousins were great hunters and went night hunting for coon and skunk. It was not to my liking and I only went with them once and felt like I had been frozen to death because this was always done in winter. There usually were enough coals left in the brush pile the next day to start the pile over again. I was surprised one time when we cut a large tree in late winter (snow on the ground) and when it fell, found a squirrel's nest with two young in a hollow of the tree. Up to that time I didn't think squirrels had young that early in the year.

In the early years on the latest farm, we burned the leaves under the trees in the woods. This was to allow grass and weed growth under the trees for pasture. We would go all around the property lines, raking the leaves away from the fences. This was to prevent the fire from spreading to the neighbors' land and to protect the fence posts from the fire. The burning was done when the leaves were damp but not wet. In the very early years, Grandpa helped and raked the leaves with a wooden rake. In later years, we still used the wooden rake and kept it hung up in the car shed. The wooden rake was great for leaves. The size of the wooden prongs kept them from impaling the leaves and clogging the rake. The height of the rake allowed a big load of leaves to be raked at one time.

Wooden Rake Like Grandpa's

Before the woods got mostly cleaned up, they were a haven for wild grapes, which, while small, were good to eat. These all went bye–bye as we gradually cleaned up the outer perimeters of the fields. Dewberries grew in the road ditches and these were absolutely delicious. There never were enough for anything but eating them as we picked them, usually on the way home from serving at Mass. One time as Dad and I were walking home from the bottom, he spotted some "June apples" on a small tree on the Meisel tract. They were red and perfect miniature apples and tasted good. I never saw them anywhere else and will probably never see them again because the land has all been cleared off.

The woods also was the general habitat for snakes. These were mostly black snakes and copperheads, although the occasional multicolored garter snake and cottonmouth showed up. Of these, the copperhead and cottonmouth were poisonous. Dad said there were quite a few rattlesnakes when the Veit family first moved to Osage Bend in 1914, but they were all gone by the time I was around. One summer, I killed two copperheads in the yard by the house. One time when I was shocking wheat in the "stump patch" I picked up a bundle and heard a hiss and saw a copperhead under the bundle. This was only the second time I heard a snake hiss. Once when I was back from Pennsylvania on vacation I was walking in the back of the big field and saw a short brownish snake. I walked to the fence row and got a stick and came back and poked the snake. It spread out its body to three times its normal width. When I poked it again, it rolled over on its back and appeared dead. I believe it was what was called a spreadhead snake which would have been poisonous. I never saw another one like it.

In the hog pasture there were very few trees so I would not call it a woods. Most of the trees were walnut and we gathered many a bushel of walnuts from them. Walnuts had a thick fairly soft outer shell which had to be removed to get to the inner shell which contained the meat. The juice in this outer shell would stain anything it contacted. In earlier centuries it was used as a dye by pioneers. The hog pasture also contained persimmon trees. One of the ditches in the hog pasture had a four-inch thick layer of white clay which I believe was what was called fire clay. There wasn't too much of it.

HOME

Water Supply

IN OUR EARLY YEARS we used cistern water collected from the roof of the house when it rained. The more high class people diverted the first water from the roof to avoid allowing the collected dirt on the roof from settling into the cistern. Although we had a diverter, we never used it, because of the risk of forgetting to set it right and losing all the rain water. Water was scarce for a large family. When we lived a quarter-mile up the road, we had a pitcher pump in the house connected to the cistern. This made it easy to get water.

When we moved down the road, the cistern was to the east of the house, off of what was then the back porch, now the kitchen and bathroom, and we had an outside pump.

Pitcher Pump

Outside Cistern Pump

When the water bucket froze over night in the kitchen, we knew it was cold enough to also freeze the cistern pump, preventing us from pumping any more water. This is where the kettle of water came in. The water was pumped out of the cistern by a rotating chain which had rubber cups every so far which would catch the water and pull it up through a pipe. Each cup had a small drain hole, so water would not stand in the pipe and freeze in the wintertime. When the weather got too cold, the top rubber cup, being wet, would freeze to the pipe and the pump could not be operated. Hence the kettle of water. The wood cook stove would have been fired up (the fire went out each night), and the kettle water heated to boiling. The kettle of hot water was then taken out to the cistern and when the top of the pump was removed, the hot water was poured down the pipe to unfreeze the cup. This worked every time, but it also created a hazard. An unwary kid, me included, would hook the kettle onto the cistern spout, hold the kettle lid in his left hand and proceed to crank the pump handle with his right. Unfortunately, the cistern top would not have been put back on and the rotating chain would catch the kettle lid and down the cistern it would go, never to be rescued. The unfortunate kid caught hell from Mom, believe me.

Water Dipper

Around 1937, my dad had a well dug on the place between the house and barn. The well diggers used, by today's standards, antique equipment. They moved in with us for a month while the well was drilled. By the way, the well was located where my grandfather Veit "witched" for water. It wound up 154 deep before it hit an inexhaustible supply of water.

The well drilling equipment consisted of a Model T engine operating a winch which raised a heavy iron bit that was then dropped about six to ten feet to crush some of the rock. The bit was pulled up and dropped time after time. After a while the bit was completely withdrawn and water poured down the hole to "dissolve" the crushed rock which was then pulled out by a dipper bucket and dumped on the ground. There was quite a pile of crushed limestone on the ground when the well was done. While one bit was in use, another was getting red-hot in a fire. When it was red it would be sharpened by hammering the drill end with sledge hammers. When the well was completed, one of the drillers took a mirror and caught the sun to shine a beam of light down the well shaft. I could see the stream of water pouring into the well so the hole must have been drilled quite straight.

Dad bought a single cylinder gasoline engine (Monitor by brand name) and a well jack to operate the pump. The engine had a cast iron container of water in the head which cooled the engine. I wonder why it never froze and cracked. Maybe we kept a piece of wood in it to absorb the stress of freezing. To start the engine, the pump had to first be disconnected which was simply done. Then, with the thumb holding down a valve stem to relieve the compression, the engine was cranked up to speed by hand and the valve released to start it. This was fine except, for a kid with a short reach, the hand holding the valve would tend to bend downward and touch the spark plug which was just below the valve. Wow! Several thousand volts and jolts!

When the engine was started, the pump drive mechanism would be engaged. The engine had a flywheel governor which disconnected the ignition when the engine tended to over speed which it did when the well pump was on the down stroke. This type of engine is called a "hit or miss" engine. The running engine had a distinct sound. It would go "pop" "pop" "pop" on the up stroke of the pump and then, coasting, would go "k-nunk" "k-nunk" "k-nunk" (a poor imitation) on the downstroke.

Typical "Monitor" Engine and Pump

The pump originally had a handle, but pumping by hand was almost impossible. An iron rod ran down a pipe from the pump 154 feet to the bottom where a flapper cup was attached. When the rod descended, the flapper opened filling the bottom part of the pump pipe with water. When the rod was raised the water forced open a higher flapper which trapped the water while the rod was lowered again. When water finally began to flow out the pump, the operator was lifting 154 feet of rod plus a 154-foot long column of water in the pipe. Quite a load.

Shortly after our well was drilled, a drought hit the area and water became scarce. Ours was the only well in the vicinity that did not go dry and the neighbors loaded their wagons up with barrels and pumped water from our well. For a while the Monitor pump ran day and night to accommodate all the people.

In 1945, after World War II, Mom and Dad decided to modernize and remodel their house. A cellar was dug under what had been the back porch and a basement poured there. This held a wood-fired furnace (with heating pipes wrapped in asbestos, a "no-no" today) and a kitchen, a bathroom, and an upstairs bedroom were built above it. The attic above the old kitchen (present dining room) was raised and made into another bedroom. A concrete cistern was poured along the back side of the house and this became the back porch area. We retained the old cistern and half the rainwater was collected in it.

My father was already working with Joe Schmidt as a carpenter then and my two oldest brothers were living in Jefferson City going to High School. So, believe it or not, the job fell to me at the age of 13 to put in all the plumbing required for the bathroom, the kitchen sink, and the pump to pump water through the system. The piping was all iron, and had to be cut to length and threaded. Thank God, Dad borrowed a vise and pipe threading tools that I could use. In my ignorance, I did not know about pipe dope for the threaded joints and had to tighten each joint excessively to prevent water leakage. I installed a diverter valve so water could be pumped alternately from either cistern. The cast iron sewer pipe for the bathroom stool ran under the basement ceiling and out through clay tile to a spot below the barn. I packed each joint with

oakum and tamped lead wool. I needed a strap to
hold up the sewer pipe up to the joists and Dad
was supposed to get one in town. Temporarily,
the pipe was held up by many strands of baling
wire wrapped around the pipe and a spike in a
basement ceiling joist. Fifty years later, after Dad
died, the strap still was not there but the baling
wire was still doing its duty as a "temporary" strap.

The new cistern had a capacity of 15,000
gallons and should have held much water.
However, before we had hooked the pipe from
the guttering to the cistern one of us looked in it
and found it had two feet of water. A spring had
broken through the floor and was flowing into the
cistern. This would have been nice, but spring
water was like well water, "hard", that is filled
with minerals and almost useless for bathing and
washing clothes. A cooking kettle in which well
water was constantly used would develop a layer
of mineral deposits as much as a quarter of an inch
thick on the inside. This acted as an insulator and
took away from the kettle's value. It was said that
keeping a marble in the kettle would prevent this,
but we never tried it to my knowledge. Hard
water also caused soap suds to curdle (even from

our homemade soap) and twice as much soap was needed. The spring could not be left in the cistern, both because of the hard water and because springs had a tendency to go dry in the summer. So we bailed out all the water and I went down into the cistern with a pipe and a batch of quick setting cement.

I knocked out the concrete around the spring, put a threaded pipe over it and cemented the hole around the pipe with the quick set. Then I screwed a cap on the pipe to close off the spring. The spring then decided to come out in the basement which was wet most of each year thereafter. As far as I know, the pipe is still in the cistern bottom holding back the spring. Long after I left the farm, Dad had another well drilled and this one went almost four times deeper than the old one, but took less than a day to drill. It has a submersible electric pump at the bottom.

Washing Clothes

WASHING CLOTHES TODAY is relatively simple. One sorts out the colors from the whites, puts a load in the automatic washer, and turns it on. When the washer completes its cycle, the clothes are transferred to an automatic dryer and it is turned on. When the dryer cycle is completed, the clothes are removed and folded up or hung up. End of job, with plenty of free time in between. Not so when I was growing up.

Before we had electricity, we had a gasoline engine-driven Maytag washing machine like the one shown below. It had a rectangular tub and a set of wringer rolls which could be rotated to different positions. The gasoline engine was an air-cooled, two-cycle, single-lunger. The pipe in the front of the machine in the picture was a flexible metal tube which was stuck through a hole in the porch wall to vent the fumes outside. The handle at the right of the wringer, when lifted, allowed the wringer to be rotated to different positions. Rotating the handle reversed the rotation direction of the wringer rolls.

Maytag Gasoline Engine-Driven Washing Machine

A handle at the left of the tub (not shown in the photo) was used to engage or dis-engage the agitator. The engine was started with a step down pedal much like today's motorcycles. That is, *if* it would start. Because of the exhaust fumes, it had to be kept on the back porch and was subjected to the cold weather which it didn't like. It took a lot of kicking and praying on those cold days to get it to start. But this came later.

First a copper boiler was placed on the wood cook stove and filled with water and the water was heated to the boiling point. Meanwhile, two galvanized wash tubs which sat on a bench next to the washing machine were filled with cold water. Bluing (don't ask me what it was, to me it was just blue fluid) was added to one tub for whitening the shirts and blouses which were washed first. When the water on the stove was hot, it was carried by the bucket out to the porch and poured into the machine tub. That's when the kicking to start the engine began.

Once the engine was started, the agitator (much like that in today's machines) was engaged and the white clothes were put in the tub. Believe me, we had a lot of white clothes despite living on the farm. It was "de rigeur" for white shirts and blouses to be worn to church on Sunday, and dish towels and bed sheets were white, as were handkerchiefs. So there were several tubs of white to be washed. The first in, of course, was the white shirts and blouses. After the machine had operated for a while (about 20 minutes), the agitator was disengaged and the wringer swung into position between the washer tub and a rinse tub. Each piece of clothing was sent through the wringer which removed most of the water and returned it to the washer tub. When this process was finished, the washer tub was refilled with clothes and the agitator put in motion.

Copper Wash Boiler

The wringer was then rotated into position between the two rinse tubs. Each piece of clothing was then rinsed up and down by hand in the first tub and then fed through the wringer into the second rinse tub which had the bluing in it. The water squeezed out by the wringer was automatically returned to the first tub. The wringer was then rotated again, this time to the side of the last tub. The clothes were again rinsed by hand up and down in the second tub and then fed through the wringer. As they exited the wringer, they were caught and placed in a basket. The white clothes were not yet ready to be hung up to dry. The shirts and blouses were dipped into a bucket of starch water, wrung out by hand, and put back in the basket. Then they were ready for hanging.

Showing How a Wringer Works

The basket of wet clothes was taken out to the clotheslines (we called them wash lines) to be hung up. Each piece was taken out of the basket, shook out to remove most of the wrinkles, and pinned to the line with clothes pins. On cold days, the clothes would freeze by the time we pinned them to the lines. This was done barehanded and, believe me, fingers got cold. It always fascinated me that frozen clothes would dry on a line, but they did. We had four lines, each about 40 feet long. By the time the clothes were hung up, it was about time to remove the next load from the washer. This went on all day to do the washing for a large family. The dirtiest clothes, namely our overalls, which picked up all the dirt from the farm work, went into the last tub.

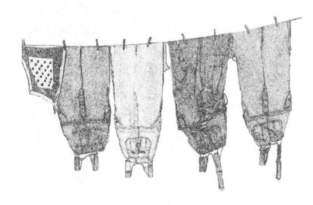

Clothes on Wash Line

Of course, the job was not yet completed. All the water in the machine had to be emptied. One could not just let it loose on the porch, so it was emptied into a bucket and carried by the bucketload out to a tree where it was poured out to water the tree. If the water was allowed to set in the machine tub for any length of time after the washing was done, the bottom water in the washer was almost mud from all the dirt removed from the clothes. Both tubs of rinse water had to be emptied also. These tubs had two handles so that when half the water had been emptied the tub could be carried outside by two people to be emptied.

Sadiron (with Removable Handle)

Now this is not the end of the story. The dried clothes had to be taken off the line and put away, which meant folding all the stuff that went into drawers. However, here was the catch. All the clothes were cotton so they wrinkled badly. This meant ironing all the handkerchiefs, dish towels, shirts, and blouses. The handkerchiefs and dish towels and sometimes pillow slips were ironed just as they came off the line with an iron heated on the wood cook stove. We had what were called "sad irons" (we never called them that), which had a detachable wooden handle. The irons were heated up on the stove and one picked up with the handle. After a bit of ironing, the iron would cool and it had to be placed back on the stove and another warm iron picked up with the handle.

The shirts and blouses were a different matter. They had been starched and hung on the line to dry. Each was gotten out and hand sprinkled with water to dampen the starch and rolled up for the water to permeate throughout. Each piece was then taken out, one at a time, unrolled and ironed and then hung on a hanger. Let me assure you, ironing a white shirt so that it has no wrinkles is not an easy task. This job was reserved for the day after the washing.

When we got electricity, nothing much changed except that the washing machine could be used inside and we didn't have to kick start the engine. I was long gone from home before Mom and Dad got an automatic washer and dryer.

Cheap Flooring

BEFORE THE HOUSE WAS REMODELED, the old kitchen had a linoleum floor which was badly worn. Mom decided to do something about it. She got some black, green, brown, and maybe yellow paint. First she painted the whole floor a green background color. Then, using pencil lines to guide us, we painted a border around it with inch-wide strips. Then we dipped crumpled newspaper in various colored paints and stippled it onto the rest of the flooring. I don't know about the rest of the family, but I thought it looked great. Today, this goes by the fanciful name of faux painting.

The floors of the rooms in the original house were of pine, tongue and grooved type, finished by painting it with plain old motor oil. When we remodeled the house, Dad borrowed a commercial sander from St. Mary's Hospital and we sanded all the floors and finished them with varnish. They couldn't compete with oak hardwood floors, but they looked okay and stayed that way for many years.

I should mention something here about cleaning floors. All the rooms got swept of course and the bedrooms got dusted with an oiled dust mop and scrubbed once in a while. However, scrubbing the kitchen floor was an every Saturday evening task. After the chores were done, supper eaten, and the dishes washed, it was time to scrub the floor. A bucket of water and a scrub rag were the tools. It also was a time for listening to the Grand Ole Opry which was broadcast every Saturday evening from WSM in Nashville, Tennessee. We heard advertisements for Duckhead work clothes that "wore like iron," Martha White flour, Prince Albert tobacco, and some kind of insurance.

The Outbuildings

THE FARM HAD A NUMBER OF OUTBUILDINGS with descriptive names. These included the barn, the machine shed (one time the old barn), the hen house, the smokehouse, the privy (outdoor), the brooder house, the well house, and the car shed. Of these, the old barn, the smokehouse, the privy, and the hen house were the only ones on the place when my parents bought it in 1936.

The privy was a ramshackle affair and Dad replaced it with an "elegant" two-holer with one hole at a low level to accommodate kids. It did not have a collection pit beneath it and had to be cleaned out periodically. An old Montgomery Ward or Sears catalog provided the toilet tissue and made fine reading while one was sitting and pondering the wonders of nature. We had the outdoor privy for a while after we installed indoor plumbing in 1945. It got moved to behind the brooder house then.

The next building my dad built was the car shed. It held one car, had a small door, two large hinged doors, and one small window. The sides were made of somewhat fancy horizontal clapboard and the roof was corrugated tin. The studs and sills were oak, where from, I do not know. The clapboard was bought at a lumber yard. Of course it was painted white.

The next year the main barn was constructed. It supplemented the old barn which was on the place when we arrived. The new barn was of hip roof construction, with hayfork provisions for putting hay in the loft. The lumber for the barn came from logs cut on the place by Dad and his brother-in-law Emil Mertens, who lived three houses up the road at the time. The lumber was sawed on the place from the logs with a rig owned by the Hoelschers. The sawing resulted in a large pile of sawdust across the road. Leo Cassmeyer would use some of the sawdust for bedding in his truck when he hauled cattle to St. Louis. We also had a large pile of slabs which came from the sides of the logs and made good kitchen firewood when sawed into lengths and split.

Left: Car Shed, Center: David Brown Tractor, Right: Hen House

The barn was designed by Joe Schmidt, the local carpenter of the time, and built under his supervision. Things were a little primitive at the time and Joe laid out the foundation with string to measure the length. Unfortunately, he used the wrong knot in the string for one side of the barn and one side of the foundation was four inches longer than the other. This was taken care of by chipping concrete off the top of the foundation. The barn was 30 feet wide and 40 feet long. It had stables on the upper (south) side as well as on the north side. A six-foot wide hall ran through the center of the barn between the stables. On the upper side, the very west "stable" was made into a granary which had a door about six feet above the concrete floor for shoveling in grain and a door to the hall where the grain could be removed. The inside was covered by boards with laths across the joints to keep grain from leaking out the cracks between the outside boards. The barn was built with "green" (uncured or dried) lumber so the siding on the outside shrank with time, leaving about one-half inch cracks between the boards. One year we sawed laths (called "lats" by us) to nail over the cracks, but very few got put in place.

Barn in Far Background; Well House in Mid-Background; Backyard Fence; and Grandchildren in Foreground

Two wooden brackets near the granary held the horse harness. The lower side of the barn was about four feet lower than the upper side so the stables on that side were correspondingly lower. Hay was pitched down into the mangers on the lower side and up into the mangers on the upper side. Most of the time the stables on the upper side were reserved for the horses and for the occasional sow with piglets. The cows were put into the lower stables.

Since the loft was above the stables, the loft on the lower side was four feet lower than the loft on the upper side. In other words, it had a split-level loft. Access to the loft was gained by a vertical ladder from the hall to the upper level of the loft, where a wider, slanted ladder went all the way up to the roof, which was quite a way up. Of course, hay, and occasionally chopped-up corn stalks (fodder) or oats straw, was stored in the loft and fed to the cows and horses in the wintertime. One time the fodder was damp when it was blown up into the barn and it fermented, getting hot and venting steam most of the winter.

There was a hayfork track with a trolley (carrier) running the length of the barn at the peak of the roof. Hay was pulled up into the loft from the wagon with a hayfork which used a one-inch thick rope.

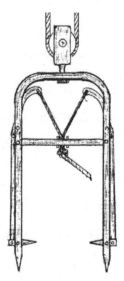

Regular Two-Prong Hayfork

This was an ingenuous contraption. The hayfork hung from the trolley on a swivel and a pulley. It had a quarter-inch rope attached to it for "tripping" the hayfork. The trip fork rope was used to pull the hayfork to the end of the barn roof (which stuck out about eight feet past the barn doors and was called the point of the barn). When the mechanism hit the end of the trolley track, the hayfork with the attached pulley would detach from the carrier and drop down to the wagon. The hay fork was pushed ("stomped") down into the hay and two levers on the fork would be pulled up, which forced two prongs toward the center of the fork, clamping the hay to the fork. Then came "hollering" to the other end of the barn to the driver of the team of horses who were connected to the other end of the one-inch rope. As they proceeded walking away from the barn, the rope would pull the hayfork load of hay up to the hayfork carrier. The moment the hayfork reached the carrier, the carrier would grab it and the whole thing, carrier and hayfork, would roll along the track into the barn. When the load reached the appropriate spot in the barn, the trip rope would be pulled, dumping the load of hay. The team driver would stop the horses, turn them around and drive them back to the original starting place. The hayfork operator would pull the fork back out of the barn and the process would be repeated until the wagon was cleared. If the wagon had been properly loaded and the hay was right, four hayfork loads would clear the wagon with hardly a wisp of hay left. When driving the team back, the driver had to hold onto the rope to keep the double tree from dragging on the ground and hitting the heels of the horses. Of course, this became an unpleasant job, if the rope had happened to drag through a pile of fresh cow poop.

To service the hayfork carrier there was a built-in ladder at one end of the loft and a platform under the roof to stand on when working on the hayfork (or changing the type of fork.) The original hayfork had two pointy prongs for pushing down into the hay. A better version, used later, was called a grapple fork. Ours had four large curved tongs which pulled into the hay as it was lifted, much like ice tongs into a cake of ice.

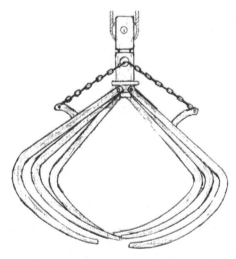

Six-Prong Grapple Fork

The platform became a delight for us kids when the hay got lower in the loft as winter progressed. We would climb the ladder to the platform and jump off down onto the hay. When the hay got low, the distance was far enough to give a freefall sensation. The peak of the roof was about 30 feet above the loft floor. If the hay had not been so resilient we would have broken our legs or necks or both. When we got electricity in 1941, the barn loft was equipped with one light, two lights were put in the hall, and one light was put in the lower stable area. This was the end of the coal oil lantern era.

The next building to arise was the well house. This was built around the well a year or two after the well was dug. It had a concrete floor and foundation and a hole through the foundation for water to drain. It had a rectangular concrete vat below the floor level that would hold up to three ten-gallon milk cans. Here is where we kept the milk until it was picked up by the milk hauler. There was a hole in the bottom of the vat which connected by a pipe to the water trough in the barn lot. There was a "riser" pipe that could be stuck into the hole to raise the water level in the vat about three-quarters of the height of a milk can. The cold well water was pumped into the vat and when the level got high enough it ran down through the riser pipe to the water trough.

One time the well house became infested by large cockroaches. When the light was turned on at night, the floor would be black with them. Amazingly, within seconds, the floor would be empty. We solved this problem by putting two box turtles in the well house. In a short time, the turtles were so fat they couldn't close their shells and the roaches were gone.

View to the North, Foreground: Kid's Rope Swing, Milk Can Lid, Background: Backyard Gate, Brooder House, Renterghem's Fields

The brooder house was the next building constructed. It was a fancy affair, with one double-hung window on each of the east and west sides and two windows and a door on the south side. The north side had a brick chimney to accommodate a heating stove to provide warmth for the chicks. The sides of the brooder house were six-inch wide, tongue in groove pine boards which made for an airtight enclosure. The ceiling was fiberboard which, unfortunately, expanded and sagged as it absorbed the vapor exhaled by several hundred chicks. The foundation extended about a foot above the ground, except for a small length on the east side where it was at ground level. A hinged door covered this gap and was used to let the chicks out into a pen when they got big enough. Writing this brings to mind a "catastrophe." My Aunt Catherine Mertens' sister and brother-in-law gave us children a cute little black and white puppy dog which we kept outside as was normal for farm dogs. One Sunday we went visiting and when we came back discovered 63 baby chickens piled up neatly in the brooder house pen. Unknown to us, the dog was a bird dog and followed his instincts. He bit the chicks in the neck which killed them and carried them to the pile. Needless to say, my parents were out of a lot of money and the dog did not live to see another sunrise. In later years my nieces and nephews and my children used the brooder house as a play house.

After this, the old barn was torn down and the lumber used to build a machine shed. The machine shed was 20 feet wide and about 30 feet long. It was open on one end and had a wide door on the south side near the back. This last door was eventually boarded up. The rear foundation was part of the stone foundation from the old barn. I helped build this shed. The only lumber we needed, besides that from the old barn, was the stringers to tie the sides of the shed and the rafters together. Dad and I found a tree that would make a 20-foot long log and had it sawed up into two-by-fours. It didn't quite make enough for one to each set of rafters, and some are missing to this day. Later a lean-to shed was added on the lower side to accommodate more machinery.

It's time to write about the smoke house. Today that sounds like a strange name for a building, but it was quite appropriate. It was used to cure and store the meat from the hogs that we butchered. Hog meat was cured by salting it down or smoking it. The smoke house had two rooms. The back room was an airtight windowless room in which the meat was hung to be smoked. The fresh meat was hung up in this room, a hickory wood fire was built on the concrete floor, the door was closed and the hickory fire smoldered for weeks and the room filled with smoke. The front room had two windows and contained the door for entering the smoke house. There was a large oaken box with a flat lid in this room. The box was about four feet wide and deep and about six feet long. In this, bacon sides, shoulders, etc. were packed in lots of salt to cure. Once cured, this meat would not spoil even in the hot summertime. Some sausage was hung on binder twine lines in the front part of the smoke house.

We also used the front room for storing odds and ends, such as the sausage grinder, sausage stuffer, and the cream separator before we sold bulk milk. It also held the old kitchen cabinets after new cabinets were installed in the remodeled house.

One summer, while back on vacation from Philadelphia, I was given the task by Mom of cleaning out the smoke house. She was going to tear it down, I guess because it was no longer needed and it was very close to the house. In cleaning it out, I discovered two sticks of badly decomposed dynamite in one of the cabinet drawers. It was left over from when I dynamited stumps while I was still at home. Decomposed dynamite produces liquid nitroglycerine, a very explosive substance that can be set off by any shock. I very carefully removed the drawer with the dynamite and carried it to a ditch below the barn and carefully buried it.

The hen house was on the place when Dad and Mom bought it. It was about 30 feet long and about 20 feet wide. It was open, but screened in at the bottom on the south side. The foundation was concrete and, being built on a bit of a hill, was low in the front and high in the back. The back was graced with a single window opening through which we pitched the chicken manure when we cleaned out the house. The front had the only door and there was one step down between it and the concrete floor. The nests were along the north side wall and there was a roost consisting of a grid of two-by-fours about two feet off the floor. The chickens roosted on this at night. It accommodated up to 300 chickens. For the life of me, I can't remember what the feeders and waterers looked like. I know we sometimes fed the chickens corn which we just threw on the ground or the floor for the chickens. Chickens were also fed oyster shells which was supposed to give them grit for their craw to grind up food, but also give them calcium for strong egg shells.

We gathered eggs once a day and of course there was more than one egg to a nest. Once in a while a broody hen would be setting on the eggs thinking she was going to hatch them and she would peck the hand that reached under her for the eggs. It really hurt. Also, once in a while a rooster would get aggressive and attack. We went barefoot in the summertime and there seemed to be no way to avoid stepping in chicken poop and having it ooze between your toes.

One time, when we were old enough to know better, my sister Mary Ann and I got into a contest to see who could hit the hen house ceiling with an egg. We busted many a one in the process. To teach us a lesson, Dad rubbed both our faces with broken eggs. Ugh!

There was a small loft with an oak floor above the hen house ceiling, with a door to the front reached by a ladder on the outside. Here is where we kids sneaked to smoke our coffee ground pipes and do other forbidden things, like read detective magazines that we sneaked from Uncle Frank. The very peak of the roof in the loft had two boards that didn't quite meet. Here the mice would run. Unfortunately for them, their tails would hang down between the boards and we would grab them and pull the mouse down between the boards. If done carefully, one could grasp the mouse behind the head, preventing a bite and kill it. There always were plenty of mice.

The roof of the hen house was corrugated metal and was nailed down with the most unusual nails I have ever seen. Each nail head was encased in lead which molded to the metal roof when it was completely driven in. I guess this was supposed to prevent leaks when it rained or when snow sat on the roof. I have never seen such nails any place else.

In early days, the purple martin house pole was attached to the front of the chicken house. It had a piece of tin wrapped around it to prevent cats and snakes from climbing the pole and eating the birds. Sparrows and martins shared the house equally, but with much squabbling. This sharing occurred despite the fact that we didn't put the house up until a few days before the martins were scheduled to arrive which they did regularly (on St. Joseph's Day I believe).

One time an extra-long black snake managed to climb the pole and we became aware of it because of the unusual clamor raised by the birds. It was too late by that time. The snake was already coming down the pole. Dad shot it with the 12-gauge shotgun as it was crossing the tin and the blast cut it in two. Both parts fell to the ground. The top part scurried under a large rock. I lifted the rock and the snake hissed at me, the only time I ever heard a black snake hiss. Where it was cut in two, little dead birds came oozing out, leaving an indelible memory for me. In later years, the martin house was moved to the rear of the car shed.

Many years later, after Dad and Mom quit raising chickens, the hen house was cleaned out and used for storage. Dad enclosed the open space on the upper side with windows. One year around New Year's, my daughter Mary Catherine, who was still at home, talked Dad into letting her use it for a party. It was cold as the devil and Dad fired up the propane heater he used on construction jobs to try to heat the place. It had no insulation, just boards between the inside and the outside weather and cracks in the ceiling up into the loft. It never did get warm and Mary's party goers had to tough it out.

Cutting the Lawn

THIS IS WORTH TALKING ABOUT because it was done differently than it is today. We had a push mower with steel wheels. The wheels had crossways grooves so that they would get traction on the grass. This was necessary because the wheels drove the rotating reel that cut the grass. The reel had about four cutting bars arranged in spirals around the center. These forced the grass against a cutting bar at the bottom of the mower. The spiral arrangement kept the grass from being cut in wavy lengths which would have looked strange. It also caused the blade to cut in a scissors fashion with a slicing motion.

We could not afford grass seed so the lawn was a mixture of grasses, mostly blue grass, but some areas consisted of what we called wire grass. Wire grass was hard to cut, being very tough and wiry instead of flat in cross-section. When we hit a patch of this, the steel wheels would tend to lose traction and the grass would clog the mower. This meant backing up, freeing the reel, and trying again.

Sheep Shears

Occasionally, we would trim the grass around the few trees. We used a "sheep shears" for this. There was no such thing as an electric or gasoline-powered edger then. We weren't smart enough to tie baling wire around the sheep shears handle to keep it from opening, and, when you then closed it, the blades would go on the wrong side of each other and it wouldn't cut. So, we had to hold it partially closed against the power of the spring-loaded handle. My brother Al called these "horse mane shears" and said they wouldn't cut a mane worth a dang. I believe him, because they were never sharp and also were not intended to cut horse's manes. However, I don't believe they would have cut a sheep's wool either.

We also could not afford machine sharpening of the push mower so it was always somewhat dull. Attempting to sharpen it would only cause the reels to miss the cutting bar and not cut the grass. My brother Roderick at one time did some part time work sharpening reel mowers with a machine. When the sharpening was finished, he could spin a sharpened blade by hand and feed paper into it and watch it just make mincemeat of the paper. Our mower never got professionally sharpened.

Cutting the grass was hard work, because pushing the mower furnished the only power for cutting. How I would have enjoyed having today's rotary mowers. Or even the gasoline engine-driven reel types that preceded them. But we didn't (the rotary mower had not yet been invented) so we got lots of exercise. My uncles

Bud and Emil came up with a rotary electric mower shortly after World War II that worked wonders, but it was too late for me.

Furniture

WE HAD AN ODD ASSORTMENT of furniture. We had three tables: a kitchen table, a dining room table, and a "hall" table. The hall table was about three feet wide and four feet long and was made of oak. It had one drawer in which Mom kept what few photographs she had. The table was strictly decorative and stayed in the front room.

The first kitchen table we had was a drop-leaf table with one loose leg. This is the first table I can remember and that goes back to when I was less than five years old. One time, my Uncle Emil and Aunt Catherine were visiting us and stayed for supper. Mom and Aunt Catherine washed up all the dishes and stacked them on the drop leaf table. My cousin Roger and I were playing on the floor and somehow knocked out the loose leg. The dishes came tumbling down and many broke. Mom bemoaned the fact that the accident happened after the dishes were washed instead of before. Dad caught hell for never fixing the leg. I don't believe he ever did.

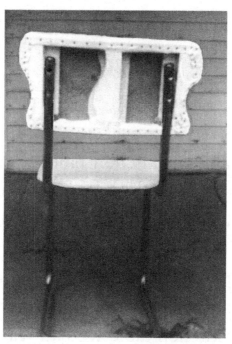

My Design for Chair Backs

The next kitchen table we had was a homemade one that seated three children to a side and an adult at each end. Three of us kids sat on a bench on one side and the bench was always turning over. When my brother Clarence went into the Navy in 1945, he bought Mom a porcelain topped kitchen table that had two leaves that could be pulled out. Mom used it the rest of her life. When I came back on vacation from Philadelphia one time my mom had me make decorative backs for the chairs (as shown in the picture below) and re-upholster them. The open back shown in the picture was also covered with material. After 35 years, the bottom of the chair legs finally wore through and they had to be discarded. My brother Rod still has the table in his "cabin" at the Osage River.

Mom had an oak dining room table with leaves and a set of oak chairs that did not quite match the table. She got them from her father and mother-in-law when she married. She still had the set when she died. It is now in the possession of my nephew, Kenneth Veit. Some of the glue joints are beginning to come apart after 75 years. Sometime in the 1960s or 1970s, I refinished the table and chairs and sprayed them with lacquer. I believe that was the last time they were refinished.

In the early days, we had a Davenport that folded out into a bed. We kids slept on that for a number of years. Mom finally took the sides off and moved it to the basement with intent to re-upholster it. She never got that done and the bare springs stayed in the basement until she died. We got beds with metal headboard and footboard. They had curved metal tube tops formed with the legs. There were vertical iron tubes for bars between the top and a crosspiece. After the house was remodeled, Mom bought a fancy bedroom set with waterfall tops. I had to re-veneer some of the tops in 1963. My sister Mary Ann has the bedroom set now.

Dresser from Mom's Bedroom Set

Mom also had a cedar chest which she got, I

believe, before she was married. She pasted important newspaper articles such as her wedding and her dad's and her brother's obituaries on the inside of the lid. It had a sort of oak finish originally, which Mom removed in 1963 and gave me the job of covering it with veneer. I did that and it looked beautiful. I don't know what happened, whether it was the gunk Mom used to remove the original finish or the veneer glue I used, but about ten years later the veneer began to peel. I redid it, although not as beautifully as at first. My sister Mary Ann also has this chest and I think the veneer is peeling again.

Mom's Cedar Chest

There was a buffet (so called) which had a large drawer all the way across the bottom to hold table linens and two doors above that to give access to shelves for storing dishes. In back of the top was a mirror about 12 inches high running the length of the buffet and a narrow shelf on top of that. To my knowledge it was never used to store linens and dishes. At Christmas we would gather moss in the woods and build a country scene including a small creche on the top of the buffet. We did it complete with miniature roads and sprigs of cedar limbs for trees. It looked great with the scene reflected in the mirror.

We had a pair of old oak chairs with embossed oak backs given to Mom by Grandma Veit. Grandma gave Mom one pair and gave another identical pair to her daughter, Bertha Braun. The Braun's set lasted only a couple of years because they put them to everyday use. The chairs dated back to the 1870s when Grandpa's sister Anna got married. Grandpa and Grandma got them when his sister and brother-in-law died of consumption in 1912. Mom kept her two chairs in the living room and used them only when she got company. A leg got broken off one of them when Dad had a stroke while eating supper with company. Uncle George, who was quite heavy, was sitting on one of the chairs and twisted in the chair to grab Dad as he fell and one of the chair legs broke. Two of the side uprights had also finally given away. Mom shipped them to me and I made two new oak uprights, fixed the leg, and refinished them. I got them after Mom and Dad both died. They sit in my living room and are now about 130 years old.

In later years, my brother Roderick made Mom and Dad a sofa and easy chair from two-by-fours and upholstered it. It looked great, but it was quite heavy.

China Cabinet I Made for Mom

When Mom had the back porch fixed up, they installed a gas log fireplace on the back porch that extended through the wall into the dining room. Mom got tired of looking at the extension and insisted that I make her a china closet with fake bottom to cover it. I drew up plans, and had Dad buy the maple lumber in Jefferson City. I came up home to Osage Bend at Thanksgiving that year and built the china closet in the kitchen while the women bustled around me baking the turkey and making other things for the meal. Believe it or not, I got the whole thing finished, shelves, fake drawers, and fake doors with real hinges in that one weekend.

Since it covers the fireplace extension into the dining room, it was left in the house when the house was sold to my cousin's daughter.

Lighting

UNTIL WE GOT ELECTRICITY at home in 1941, we used both coal oil lamps and lanterns. Our coal oil lamps were utilitarian and were plain glass. Some people had coal oil lamps that were also decorative, being made of colored glass or with painted decorations on them. We went through too many lamps to be able to afford the decorative kind.

For some strange reason, a coal oil lamp would occasionally start to burn down inside the coal oil reservoir. This was a dangerous situation because the glass reservoir could break from the heat and spread burning coal oil inside the house. Whoever noticed it immediately grabbed the lamp and ran outside and threw it in the grass. This often put out the fire but broke the lamp.

In the 1880s, the German newspaper "Volksfreund" of Jefferson City recommended dumping flour on a kerosene lamp fire to put it out.

Lamps had detachable glass chimneys which had to be lifted to light the wick. Carelessness led to numerous broken chimneys and we usually had a spare or two on hand. The chimneys got coated on the inside with soot and the light would be reduced so they had to be cleaned periodically. Old newspaper did an excellent job here.

Typical Kerosene Lamp

When we had to go to the barn at night, we used a kerosene lantern. It operated in a manner similar to a kerosene lamp. However, it vented through a metal top and the glass was much thicker and was protected by metal wire. A handle was pushed down to lift the glass and permit lighting the wick.

We had a chrome metal lamp with a circular wick which ran around the top inside the chimney. This put out much more light but we seldom used it, maybe because it consumed more coal oil than an ordinary lamp or because the circular wicks were hard to find or expensive. This lamp eventually wound up in the chicken house and ultimately in the ditch across the road where one of my nephews destroyed it by throwing rocks at it. I didn't know, and am still not sure, that this type of lamp is called an Aladdin lamp.

Mom and Dad got two gasoline lamps for wedding presents. These used white gasoline which was pressurized in the tank and burned white hot in one or two asbestos mantles. They never got used at a time when I could remember, because the mantles were always broken. I thought that these were called Aladdin lamps.

Camping lanterns using mantles are in common use today.

Kerosene Lantern

In 1939, when the REA first came through, they were originally surveying to put the main line along the road by our farm. Because of the many curves in the road this would have caused many anchors to be placed in our fields. Dad convinced them that it would be simpler to run the line straight along the north line fence and run a line up to the house. For allowing them to do this, he got the line run up to the barn and house and got paid $126 and some odd cents to cut the trees from the right-of-way. Interestingly enough, all the trees were on our neighbor George Koelling's land, but if I remember right, we got the wood. Koelling insisted that the poles be on our side of the line because he was afraid that the creosote would harm his cattle.

Although the line was there in 1939, my parents didn't feel they could afford to hook up to it until 1941. The bill for 40 kilowatt-hours was $1.25 per month. With only a few light bulbs and one electric motor to run the well, 40 kilowatt-hours was about all that was used in a month.

Not everyone wanted electricity and many people did not sign up at first. One of these was Dad's cousin, Mary (Veit) (Bellman) Harrison. She would not give permission for the line to cross her land, blocking access for electricity to the farm of her brother, Joe Veit, who wanted electricity. REA had to run a mile of line on an alternate route to get electricity to her brother. When Mary finally changed her mind and wanted to be hooked up to REA, the company made her pay for the mile of line.

The Kitchen Stove

THE KITCHEN STOVE was a remarkable device whose merits were largely taken for granted. Massive and fabricated of cast iron, it combined the features of a cooking range, a food warmer, an oven, and a water heater. The front burners, over the firebox, were used for cooking. Lids could be removed with a special lid-lifter if the cook wanted to bring the cooking utensil into direct contact with the flame. A large surface, perhaps four square feet, to the right of the firebox and over the oven, was suitable for simmering.

The "front" burners were really at the side (end) directly above the fire box. There was a grate on the side that allowed adjustment of the amount of air getting to the fire, and this helped regulate the heat somewhat. The bottom of the fire box contained a grate that could be rocked back and forth with a crank to dump the ashes down into a removable collection bin. The flame and the heat traveled to the right from the fire box over the oven, down the side of the oven, across the bottom, and exited up the chimney through a hole below the oven at the back of the stove.

Kitchen Wood Stove Like Ours

Ashes collected above and below the oven, and had to be removed periodically. The ashes on top were removed simply by lifting the top lids and scooping it up. The bottom ashes were raked out through a small opening at the stove front below the oven.

Metal closets, suspended several feet above the cooking surface, and heated by the flue pipe, kept food warm. The deluxe models had a reservoir at the end opposite the firebox, in which water was heated. Water was poured in through a large, hinged lid on top. The hot water was tapped from a faucet behind a normally closed door. The reservoir also stored heat, of course.

We were not rich enough to have the deluxe model with the water reservoir so we always had a tea kettle of water on the top of the stove. We also kept the 12- or 15-cup "granite" (porcelainized) coffee pot on top of the stove. There was no such thing as a percolator or a "Mr. Coffee." Coffee grounds were just dumped into the pot and water added and it was left to simmer all day. As the pot got empty, more water, and sometimes more coffee grounds, were added. The used grounds were not emptied until they began to interfere with the amount of coffee that could be made. The coffee makings came in the form of beans which the buyer had to grind to his liking at the grocery store.

Coffee Pot Like Ours

The fire box was small and could not keep coals alive overnight. So the fire had to be started every morning, and for a number of years the job fell to me. It took paper, kindling, fine wood, and a little coal oil to get it started. I never had the advantage of Raymond's coal oil soaked corn cobs—an excellent idea that I wish I had thought of. Another job involving the stove that fell to me was baking homemade bread. I don't remember having any trouble with keeping the right temperature for the task.

One never *ever* poured kerosene on a fire or coals. My cousin Edna Imhoff found this out when she got severe burns on an arm by pouring kerosene on a fire that she thought was out.

While we are on the subject of cooking, I might mention pots, pans, and skillets. There was essentially no aluminum, so most of our pots were of the "granite" type. They were made of very thin metal which was covered with fused-on porcelain inside and out. They had a problem, in that, if they were dropped, the porcelain would chip. Once chipped, it was just a matter of a short time before the thin metal would be eaten through and a hole would develop. We plugged such holes with twisted bits of rag cut very short on the inside. The outside rag, exposed to the fire, would burn very short, but liquid in the pot kept it from burning completely. These plugs would last quite a while.

Our dishpan, which got its name from being

used to wash dishes, was also of the "granite" variety. There was no such thing as a kitchen sink. The dishpan did double duty, being used also for bread dough when we baked bread. The bread pans themselves were of cheap steel and would rust quickly if not thoroughly dried. The skillets were all of cast iron. Teflon had not been invented so there was no such thing as a non-stick pan. We had a cast iron waffle iron that had two spiral-wound wire handles for separating the two halves. It had a round knob opposite the handles which allowed it to be turned over to brown both sides of the waffle. We seldom used it; instead, we just fried pancakes in a skillet.

Making Molasses

FOR A NUMBER OF YEARS we cooked molasses. We mixed it with the old dry peanut butter to make an acceptable spread for homemade bread that we took as sandwiches to school. By springtime, the molasses would begin to settle out as sugar.

Dad and his brother-in-law George Braun owned both the cooking pan and the cane press. He built a concrete foundation on which the pan sat about two and a half feet from the ground. The pan was about four feet wide and 10 or 12 feet long and around four inches deep. It was stored above the ceiling in Uncle George's car shed when it was not being used. I have no idea what happened to the cane press. Recently, I asked my cousin Dave Braun about the pan and he said it still hangs in the old car shed, but has a couple .22 rifle holes in it from shooting at sparrows.

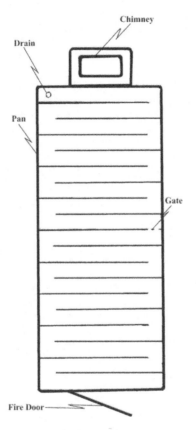

Top View of Molasses Cooker

The pan had crossways dividers every six inches along its length. A divider ran from one side to within six inches of the other side. From that side the next divider would run back to within six inches of the first side. In this manner the molasses juice was forced to travel nearly 50 feet to flow the 12 feet from one end to the other. Half way down the pan was a gate across one of the six-inch gaps that could be closed. A fire was built from the front to about half-way under the pan. The flames and heat traveled under the pan toward the rear and vented out a chimney.Raw juice was introduced at the front end and the juice traveled toward the rear, being cooked as it traveled along. As it cooked near the front, a green scum would form on the top of the juice and this was removed with a screen type scoop that just fit between the six-inch dividers. We never ate any of this because we were told that it would give us the "runs." My wife says that she and her sister would eat some of it when her relatives cooked molasses. By the time the molasses got to the gate, it was relatively free of scum.

My uncle George was the judge of when the molasses was done. Cooked too much and it would caramelize into sugar, cooked too little and it would spoil. When the molasses at the rear was ready, the gate at the midpoint would be closed and the done molasses would be drawn out of a hole at the rear of the pan. As most of the molasses at the rear of the pan was removed the gate was opened, allowing a new batch into the rear part.

The cane press had three big vertical rollers and was operated by a team of horses walking around in a circle around the press. They had to be stopped every time the operator needed a new stack of cane to put through the press. The juice was caught in a galvanized wash tub.

Raising cane for molasses was a pain. It had to be cultivated like corn, but it grew up to eight feet tall. When it was ready to harvest, all the leaves had to be stripped from the stalks. This was done with wooden "corn knives." A regular knife could not be used because it would cut into a stalk when it hit a leaf. The leaves were sharp and one got many arm cuts if a short-sleeved shirt was worn.

After it was stripped of leaves, it had to be cut with a regular corn knife, near the ground so none of the stalk would be wasted. It then had to be loaded onto a wagon to be hauled to the press. The stripped cane stalks had a powdery substance on their surface and were as slick as the devil. This made them hard to carry to the wagon and hard to hold on the wagon while it was being hauled. Molasses cane used up a lot of nutrient from the soil and could not be planted in the same place the next year.

Refrigeration

IN THE DAYS BEFORE ELECTRIC and/or gas refrigerators, folks had to find other ways to keep food cool.

Homes that were situated near a spring would erect a building over the spring. The water from the spring, flowing through, would cool the entire structure. People used spring houses to store milk, butter, and the like. The most perishable items might be placed in containers that were set directly into the fresh flowing spring water.

Our springs were too far away from the house to be used for refrigeration. We did have well water which we used to keep the milk that we sold in bulk cool.

Almost every house had a food cellar, an underground room that stayed around 50 to 55 degrees year round. We used the cellar under our house for potatoes, sauerkraut, fried-down meat, and canned food.

Even after we got electricity, we did not get a refrigerator. I think my parents bought their first one after I finished college. There is a tale told by my uncle, Frank Veit, who worked at the Montgomery Ward store in Jefferson City. He told of one of our neighbors, Henry Hollander, who refused to get electricity. Henry saw a gas refrigerator (yes, there were such things) at Montgomery Ward with a light that lit up when the door was opened. He bought it, but, then wanted to return it because the light did not go on when it was in his house.

Heating

THE MOST COMMON HEATING FUEL was wood, harvested on the farm. Most of the wood was cut into 15-inch lengths, split into pieces about the diameter of a fist, and burned in a kitchen stove. This not only heated the kitchen area but also provided fuel for cooking. Some wood was used in heating stoves, which accommodated larger, unsplit blocks of wood; usually this was done only on the coldest of winter days. Our heating stoves were rarely used; only when someone was sick, there was a new baby in the house, or we had baby chicks in an upstairs bedroom. Splitting the wood for the cook stove was not an easy task. The stove, kept burning all day, used up a lot of wood. Each big block of wood had to be split with an axe into much smaller pieces. Any hint of a knot in the wood made it difficult to split and we tried to sort out such pieces. Nevertheless, they would show up and the axe would stick in the wood instead of going all the way through.

After the wood was split, it still had to be carried from the wood pile (which never seemed to be close to the house) and stacked on the porch. We would have several rows of this wood probably six feet high. We had to allow for bad days, like severe snow storms, when splitting wood would be impossible.

I will tell one on me here. One time my brother Rod and I carried in stove wood and Rod began to tease me, which I could never stand. I got mad and threw a stick of wood at him. The sucker ducked and the wood went through a glass window, to my sorrow when Mom showed up. A replacement window cost 85¢ and could only be bought in Jefferson City.

I replaced a number of windows, not all broken by me. One time we had our potatoes in the upstairs bedroom and my brothers Clarence and Rod got into a potato throwing fight with our cousin Francis Veit. Naturally, one of the potatoes went through a window.

When the house was remodeled, we installed a wood-fired furnace and had central heating. This took much more wood so the upstairs bedroom vents were usually shut off. The furnace included a pipe loop that was supposed to furnish hot water in the wintertime. All the heating pipes were wrapped in asbestos paper by us. Wonder why none of us has yet died of lung cancer. In much later years, long after I was gone from home, a new wood-fired furnace was installed and it would switch to a propane tank if it ran out of wood. This was convenient because if wood was later added it would be lit by the propane.

There were a number of different heating stove types. Ours had an oval shape when viewed from above and had removable rails along each side for putting your feet on (with shoes of course) to warm them. The stove pipe came out of the top rear and of course went to the chimney. There were two doors on the front, a large one for putting wood into the stove and a smaller one below it for removing the ashes. The ash door had an adjustable (screw in or out) vent with which the air to the fire was regulated. Careless regulation of the air could cause the fire to burn too hot and turn the stove red and possibly catch the chimney on fire. A chimney fire was dangerous because the chimney could crack from the heat and set the house on fire. We had such a chimney fire at our old place up the road when our baby sitter put too much wood in the fire. The fire was extinguished by climbing on the roof and throwing salt down the chimney.

Stove Like Emil Hirschman's

Emil Hirschman had a different type of heating stove in his general store. It was relatively narrow and long and had only one door on the front. The locals would gather around the stove in the evenings at the store and swap tall tales. I found a picture of such a stove and include it here.

The Whippoorwill

IN THE SPRING, we anxiously listened for the first call of the whippoorwill. We knew that when the whippoorwill called, it was time to go barefoot. About the only time we wore shoes during the summer was when we went to church, went visiting, or went walking in the woods where there might be black locust thorns or other perils to the feet. After our feet toughened up, we could run on the gravel road with no problem. I'd like to say we went barefoot because we preferred it, but poverty was the real reason. We were growing up during the Depression and shoes for the whole family was an expensive affair. We got all the mileage we could get out of our shoes. They were handed down to a younger kid as the older one outgrew them. They were resoled and re-heeled and sometimes held together with baling wire.

Of course, we didn't wear these patched-up shoes to church. We had to keep up appearances. Dad had a shoe last with interchangeable "shoes" for the different shoe sizes. New soles were tacked onto the shoes after they had been placed over the last. The steel of the last clinched over the nails so that our feet were not injured as we wore them.

That was the theory. In actuality, one or two nails would not get completely clinched over and a sore would develop on the foot. This called for a return to the shoe last.

Shoe Last

Talking about going barefooted brings to mind the following poem by John Greenleaf Whittier:

Blessings on thee, little man,
Barefoot boy, with cheeks of tan!
With thy turned-up pantaloons,
And thy merry whistled tunes;
With thy red lip, redder still
Kissed by strawberries on the hill;
With the sunshine on thy face,
Through thy torn brim's jaunty grace;
From my heart I give thee joy, —
I was once a barefoot boy!

The Telephone

WE HAD A TELEPHONE when we lived up the road, but I don't remember anything about it. When we bought Grandpa and Grandma Veit's place down the road, Dad gave them our telephone to use. It stayed in the house, even after Grandpa and Grandma were gone and Uncle Frank bought the place. It went out into Uncle Frank's car shed when he got a new phone. I didn't see it there until it had been ruined by water coming into the garage.

The telephone had battery power for the microphone, but used hand power for signaling. There was a hand crank on the side which drove a magneto which put out the signaling power. The line output for signaling was 110 volts at 10 cycles per second which was enough to ring every bell connected to the line. Being the same voltage as that used to power lights and such, it was enough to knock one on his butt if he touched the line when someone was cranking. There were no such things as lightning protectors, so every phone owner disconnected his phone from the line when a storm arose. It was a favorite juvenile trick to watch out the window as someone picked up the line to reconnect it, and then turn the crank, and of course run and hide.

Signaling was done by cranking the magneto in a distinctive pattern. A ring consisted of one to four rings. A short ring, followed by three long rings meant Henry Siebeneck, for instance. Two longs and two shorts might be Emil Rackers, and so forth. The number of people who could be accommodated in this manner was limited, so the line was broken up into sections. Ours covered from Osage Bluff, five miles away, to Renterghem's. Renterghem's was an exchange point. If one wanted to talk to someone on the lower road, such as Ernie Braun, Renterghem's had to be called first. Alma Renterghem would then ring Ernie Braun and, if he answered, connect the two lines together. She had to listen to find out if the connection was still needed and disconnect the two lines when the conversation ended. Of course, there was no privacy.

What Our Telephone Looked Like

The line consisted of a single galvanized solid wire line strung from post to post with the ground acting as the return path. Each person had to furnish the posts along his property line. Since the line ran on our side of the road, Dad had to furnish poles for a half-mile of line. These were cut from oak trees, with the bark left on them. Of course, they rotted or were attacked by termites and had to be replaced periodically. The line was restrung every four or five years. One year, when new posts were set in the spring, it was extremely wet and the new posts sprouted limbs. They looked strange.

When the REA brought electricity, there was talk of putting the line on the electric poles, but this never came to fruition because the "hum" caused by induction from the power lines into the single wire would have overwhelmed the signal. No one knew that using two lines would have canceled out the hum.

My folks did not get a telephone until I was out of college and in Philadelphia. Then a company, headquartered in Brazito, Missouri, installed poles and put in a good system. It was later replaced by underground cable placed under the gravel county road.

More about Furniture

I FORGOT TO MENTION several items of furniture, mainly because we didn't use them everyday. One was the Victrola that we had in the attic. It came from Grandma Mertens and I believe belonged to her. It had a set of 78 rpm celluloid records with a wide variety of songs. It didn't work very well because, if you wound it fully, it would slip some kind of gear and unwind it self. It could only be wound part way, enough to play about one record.

In my venturesome ways, I took it apart to find the problem. The problem lay in a casing that surrounded the springs (it had two.) The casing was held onto a large round gear with screws that screwed into tapped holes in the gear. The threads in the gear were stripped and when the springs were wound too tight, the gear would tilt and rotate, unwinding the springs. Three or four small screws with nuts would have solved the problem, but I didn't have access to a hardware store, and the thing never got fixed.

Seth Thomas Mantle Clock

Mom also had a Seth Thomas mantel clock that had chimes. Needless to say, it was mechanical in nature and had to be wound periodically. To do this, the front door (the glass covering the dial) was opened and a big key was used to wind both the chimes and the clock itself. It quit working, and wound up in the attic. This was too much for my curiosity and I got it out and took it apart. The problem was that the spring on which the pendulum was suspended had broken. I fashioned a new one out of a watch spring from a cheap watch that Dad had discarded and got it working again. Unfortunately, the new spring was much stronger than the old one and the clock would not run long before it had to be rewound. The clock wound back up in the attic. I wish I had the thing today, so I could fix it right.

I don't believe I mentioned the washstand we had at first. It consisted of two wooden orange crates (rather thin wood) fastened together. Mom made a curtain that could be slid back along a string to surround it. I can't remember what the top was made of. This served our purposes until Dad finally found a marble-topped washstand that he bought for $24. Mary Ann tells me that Mom and Dad sold it for the sum of $1 while they were remodeling their house.

There was one other piece of equipment that might be classed as furniture. That was the galvanized wash tub that served us as a bath tub. The tub was filled half full with cold water and then water heated on the wood cook stove top was poured in to bring the water to a bearable temperature. I never knew why, but the girls got their baths first and then came the turn for us boys. It wasn't a comfortable place to take a bath because of its size and we didn't soak in it, even if

Mom would have let us. When finished, we got out and shivered by the wood stove until we got dried off.

Making Soap

WE MADE OUR OWN SOAP for washing clothes and dishes, and sometimes ourselves. We accumulated lard, bacon grease, and bits of meat scraps as the year went by. When we had collected enough, we put it all in a large cast iron kettle that sat on a three-legged stand under which we built a fire. Numerous cans of lye were added to the kettle and the whole batch cooked for hours. The result was a dirty brown liquid. I have no idea how much lye was used per gallon.

After the mixture had cooked long enough, we used a strainer to dip out any residual meat scraps and bones and let the kettle cool. As the liquid soap cooled, it solidified, and we then used a large knife to cut it up into bars. Needless to say, the bars were not very symmetrical, but they didn't have to be. The soap was slow to dissolve and sometimes we cut chips off of it to speed the process. However, a bar of it was just thrown into the hot water used for clothes washing.

The Houses

MY FOLKS FIRST LIVED IN A HOUSE AT TAOS on the old Veit home place. It still stands today. I think the main part is a log structure.

The Veit House at Taos Circa 1928

My grandfather added two rooms, but coming from Germany, built them somewhat in the German fashion. Instead of the German stone between the wood, he poured concrete between the studs. In 1986, Dad and I talked to the occupant, and he said it was impossible to hang a picture on those walls and the rooms were extremely cold in winter. The next house my folks had was a story and one-half house with front and back porches across the length of the house. There was a stairs up to the attic with a door at the bottom in the kitchen. The attic was unfinished but had three dormer windows across the front. It was typical clapboard construction. There was a set of steps down to the cellar, also from the kitchen. These were the set of steps that my sister Mary Ann went down in her walker. Fortunately, with no injury. The back porch was screened in. The front porch was seldom used, nor was the living room in the front used very often. There was a car shed with a separate room with a concrete floor and a barn. The barn was unusual in that it had pine siding and didn't have the cracks between the boards that barns with oak siding had. I can't imagine why anyone would build a barn with pine siding. I thought at one time that Dad did, but my older brothers assure me that he didn't. I don't know for sure, but I would assume that the back porch held the cream separator and the gasoline engine Maytag washing machine. The yard was fenced in with high woven wire and gates led to the front road, the barn, and the garden which was on the upper west side.

When I was going on five years old, Dad and Mom bought the farm down the road from Dad's dad. The house was much bigger than the old one. It had two bedrooms and an attic upstairs and a bedroom, living room, kitchen, and back porch downstairs. It was unusual in that each downstairs room had three doors into it. There was a big front door from the porch, opening onto a small hall from which the stairs went directly up to the upper bedrooms and doors went into the bedroom and the living room. There was a closet downstairs under the steps and doors led from the front of this to the bedroom and the living room. There was also a closet in the southwest upstairs bedroom. The upstairs closet had broken panels in the door and rumor was that this was from a burglary long before we got there. The back porch had a concrete floor and was screened in. Doors led from it into the kitchen and the bedroom. A wooden sidewalk led from the porch to the outdoor cistern on the east side. Concrete steps led from the back porch down to the cellar which was under the kitchen. These steps had a big wooden door level with the porch floor that had to be flopped open to get to the cellar.

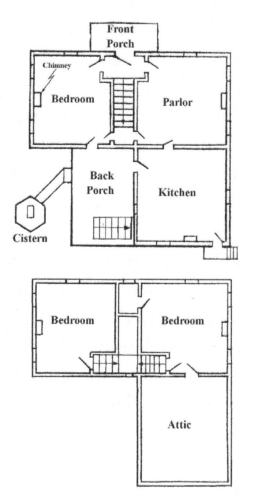

Layout of House before Remodeling

The stairs to the upper floor had walls on both

sides and, of course, at the bottom were almost two stories high. We boys would spread-eagle ourselves between the two walls and work our way to the top. We did this barefoot so we did not leave any marks on mom's wallpaper. We also slid headfirst down the steps on our bellies.

There was a landing at the top of the stairs where they branched off to the left and right to the two upstairs bedrooms with three steps each way. Sometimes a kerosene lamp was left burning on the landing so we could see upstairs. We did not have any lamps in the bedrooms. In the winter, we slept three to a bed under a feather bed (actually a feather tick) and froze until the ticking cover of the feather bed warmed up. The roof was rusted tin and the upstairs bedrooms got unbearably hot in the summertime. Then we would sleep on the floor under a window, hoping for a breeze to blow through the window which it never did unless there was a thunderstorm and then we had to shut the window. There were only two maple trees on the west of the house to shade it and these were dying of old age. Mom planted a bunch of maples from the bottom in the yard on the east side and they are still there today.

The attic was somewhat of a treasure house. It had a floor on only the center part of it and the ceiling plaster of the kitchen was visible where it had been pushed between the cracks of the plaster laths. The attic held the old Victrola, Mom's gas iron, her mantle lamps, her mantel clock, stray books, etc. There was a book by Zane Grey that frustrated me. The beginning and, more importantly, the ending were missing.

The kitchen held the wood cook stove, the kitchen table at which we ate, a makeshift wash stand, and a box for the stove wood. The floor was linoleum. All the floors in the other rooms were oil-soaked pine. The back porch floor was concrete and there we stored our stove wood and the Maytag washing machine. When washing was done, the bench we boys used to sit on at the kitchen table held the two wash tubs of water. I guess on those days we stood when we ate.

In 1945, Mom and Dad began to remodel the house. The back porch was torn off and the area under it was dug out. This formed a basement and a furnace was put in it and we had central heat. The roof was raised above the attic and another bedroom was added there. The area above the new basement contained a new kitchen and a bathroom and a small dormer bedroom upstairs. I got to do all the plumbing for the new water system that was added. A big cistern was added along the backside and the top of the cistern formed the floor for a porch. The porch had a cinder block railing with a concrete top. A few years later, just before my brother Roderick got married, I enclosed the back porch with 24 double-hung windows. His wedding dinner was held on the back porch.

Front of House before Final Remodeling, April 1951

The stairs were rerouted, to come up from the

dining room (the former kitchen). The lower part of the stairs was made out of red cedar from a tree Dad and I cut down at the bottom land. The two inch lumber was hauled to Elston, Missouri where it was turned into posts for the railing. One big newel post was also turned out of the lumber. I installed the cedar steps and this included making the top hand rail which curved at the bottom to fasten to the newel post. Years later, when the house was again remodeled and the stairs rerouted, Mom gave me the cedar lumber. I made her a floor lamp from the newel post. From the small posts I made a floor lamp for my sister Mary Ann and one for myself. From the leftover scraps I made each of my children a clock or a lamp.

The front porch was eventually enlarged to run across the whole house (this was after I was gone from home) and hardwood floor was laid in place of the old pine. The outside of the house was covered with sandstone and new windows were added. My sister Mary Ann made new drapes and hangings for the windows to Mom's design. The effect was beautiful. Roderick built a stone fireplace in the living room, but it was so pretty that Mom never used it so that it would not be blackened by smoke. I built a half-fake china closet to cover the gas log fireplace that extended into the dining room from the back porch.

FAMILY

The Garden

MOM ALWAYS HAD A GARDEN in which we raised vegetables for eating fresh and for canning. The garden was to the east of the house and was originally separated from the yard by a woven wire fence. There was a flower bed on the garden side of the fence. In the spring Dad would spread cow manure on the garden and would then plow and harrow it with the team of horses. Thinking back on it, the spreading of cow manure was a dumb thing to do, but probably all we could afford. With the cow manure came all the weed seeds the cows had eaten and we always had to fight the weeds all summer.

Mom would plant peas, beans, cabbage, cucumbers, spinach, lettuce, radishes, carrots, tomatoes, and beets. Sometimes turnips, squash, watermelon, cantaloupe , and eggplant would be added. The cantaloupe usually was of the banana variety, that is, long instead of ball shaped. After Dad had harrowed the ground we would go over it again with hoes to break up any remaining clods. The rows for planting the vegetables would be laid out. A length of binder twine with a stick on each end would be stretched from one end of the garden to the other. A small furrow would be traced along the string and in this we planted the seeds. The seeds would first be covered with good black dirt from the straw pile manure and then some of the regular dirt would be placed over top this.

Hoeing the Garden

When the plants came up, then the hoeing would start. We hoed in between the rows and carefully pulled any weeds that grew in between the plants. Hoeing was necessary because the ground would dry out rapidly if it had a hard crust so, after each rain, hoeing was necessary again.

Often, the tomato plants and the hill plants such as watermelon would have a tin can, with the bottom punched full of holes or cut out, inserted into the ground beside the plant. This would facilitate watering such plants which needed a lot of water. Radishes were usually the first thing to be ready to eat, which of course we ate raw. Next would come the lettuce, followed closely by the peas. The lettuce was of the broad leaf variety and was served with a hot grease and vinegar dressing. I didn't like it that way and still don't. Give me iceberg lettuce any day.

The peas were a pain in the butt because they had to be shelled, and shelling 50 pints of peas is a monumental task. Dad once bought a hand-cranked pea sheller which had two small rubber rolls which squeezed the peas out of the pod as the pods were fed between the rollers. It was poorly made and gave out before one-half of the crop was shelled. Looking back, I can see how I could have fixed the sheller but I didn't think of it at the time. I once talked Mom into letting me try using the washing machine wringer as a pea sheller. It worked great, except we had to put up bed sheets to catch the peas because they popped out of the pods all over the place. But it was a heck of a lot easier than doing it by hand. We would can around 50 pints of peas.

Then there were the beans. There were sometimes two varieties, yellow and green. Both were treated the same. When the bean pods had filled out, they were picked off the plants, leaving the immature beans to ripen for later. The stems and tips were cut off and the bean snipped or snapped into short lengths. They were then canned by the hot pack method. In later years a pressure cooker was used. I don't think many people use a pressure cooker today, unless they can food or live at high altitudes. The pressure cooker operated at around 15 pounds per square inch pressure which allowed the water to reach a temperature much higher than 212 degrees Fahrenheit. Bean stalks produce over a long period of time so this was an every week task, picking, preparing and canning them. I don't remember for sure, but I think we put up about 50 quarts of them.

At first, we used two types of cans (really glass jars) for canning. One had a glass lid that was held down atop a rubber washer by a metal spring on the jar. These were expensive, and as they broke we replaced them with Mason jars. These had a thread molded in the glass and the lid screwed down, squeezing the sealing rubber between it and a glass lip. The lids were zinc and after the food was canned, but still hot, we hammered the lid edge down upon the rubber with a table knife to ensure a good seal. Later, "Patent" lids came out. These fit the same jars but contained a molded-in rubber which sealed on the top edge of the jar. They were held down in the canning process by metal screw bands which could be removed and reused once the canned food had cooled.

Carrots had to be pulled out of the ground when they got big enough, but before they got too big and turned into wood. The skins had to be scraped off these and this was an unpleasant task also, especially since Mom came from the old school and wanted all the skin and none of the basic carrot removed. This precluded peeling the carrot with a knife or potato peeler. Instead, they were scraped with a paring knife held perpendicular to the carrot. I don't remember if the carrots were sliced crossways or lengthwise for canning, but I know they were sliced in some way.

Canned Food

Some years, Mom raised lima beans on the back fence of the garden. They were a climbing variety of bean and weren't picked until the pods had turned brown. The beans were then shelled out of the dry pods and canned or dried. I positively hated them.

Cabbage grew in heads which were dearly loved by worms which would eat holes in the heads. So they were always carefully checked every couple of days. When the heads got big enough, about eight to ten inches in diameter, they were cut off. These heads were cut into wedges from top to bottom and the hard core at the base of the head removed. The wedges were crammed into glass mason jars and canned with essentially no seasoning. I dearly loved eating the cabbage cold just as it came out of the jar, although we often heated it up in milk gravy for eating. We also used some cabbage to make sauerkraut. A cabbage head would be quartered and the heart cut out. The heart was tough but not too bad when eaten raw. The cabbage quarters would then be cut into thin slices with a slaw cutter.

Slaw Cutter

The slaw cutter had a wooden box which slid in slots along the side and allowed the cabbage to pass over an embedded knife which did the cutting. Mom would make one or two ten-gallon crocks of kraut. The sliced cabbage was packed in layers with each layer being liberally salted. A round wooden lid held down by a rock was placed on top of each crock. The cabbage would ferment in the salt and give off a terrible stench. After it fermented for a while, it was removed from the crock and then washed in clear water to remove the salt. It was then canned.

Cucumbers were handled in several ways. When they were picked small, they were canned whole with seasoning and called pickles. They were canned with at least two types of seasoning and one of these was called "bread and butter." We never made dill pickles. To my knowledge we never sliced any pickles before canning them. If they were allowed to become larger, they became the real cucumbers. For summertime eating we would pick a couple, peel them, slice them into a vinegar type seasoning and eat them raw. Later in the year we picked them, peeled them, removed the seeds, and sliced them lengthways in about one-half inch wide strips. These were canned in a sweet vinegar sauce and we called them "slickers," I guess because they slid down your throat easily when you ate them. They were served cold out of the can and were one of my favorites.

The spinach was picked, the leaves washed, and any bug-eaten parts cut out. The remainder was canned whole. As it was cooking in the canning process, it shrank many-fold and the finished jar would appear half empty or, as the optimist would say, half full. As a kid it was not a favorite of mine, but I dearly enjoy it now that I am aged.

The lettuce and radishes of course were only eaten fresh out of the garden and never canned.

Tomatoes were a favorite crop. They were prone to being afflicted by tomato caterpillars which, if left unchecked, would eat all the leaves off a plant. These caterpillars were huge, bright green, and had a horn on one end. We picked them off and squashed them with our bare feet. Mom said that when she was small and her parents were in the tomato raising business, they picked them off and dropped them into a can of kerosene. When tomatoes were ripe they could be picked and eaten warm (summertime) right in the garden. Otherwise, if they weren't canned, they were picked, washed, and sliced for eating raw. We would eat them two ways, with salt and pepper or with sugar. For canning, the ripe ones were picked and scalded in hot water which allowed the thin peel to be easily removed. They were then cut up and canned in mason jars. A great dish was a skillet casserole (we never called it that) consisting of liver sausage, canned tomatoes and egg noodles. In the fall, when frost threatened the unripened tomatoes, they were picked green and run through the sausage grinder which cut them up into fine chunks. These, along with raisins, were then cooked and canned. For some reason we called this "mince meat" although it wasn't. It tasted pretty good.

Beets of course grew in the ground and would get two to three inches in diameter at which time they were pulled up. The tops and root tips were cut off and the beet would be sliced crossways and canned in a vinegar sauce. The juice was essentially a dye and when canning beets, everything, hands, utensils, bowls, towels, etc., would gain a red hue. I detested them and still do.

Turnips were a mixed bag as far as I was concerned. If they were pulled up and eaten raw in the fall of the year they were delicious. We would stop by the garden on our way home from school and pull one up and eat it raw. As far as I am concerned, when turnips are cooked, as they were for canning, they taste awful and for my money should be thrown away.

Watermelon, cantaloupe, and squash were never canned. The first two were eaten just as they came out of the garden, while the squash was usually baked or fried before being eaten. There were many varieties of squash such as pumpkin, acorn, spaghetti, etc. We seldom raised eggplant. When we did, it was eaten fresh out of the garden, sliced, dipped in batter, and fried.

I almost forgot to mention potatoes because they were not raised in the garden. They were always planted in a patch across the road. The year they redid the county road, we had to move many of the plants because the road was going to take them. We raised potatoes for both food and sale. At one time I know we got 90¢ for 100 pounds. I don't remember when we first started to sell potatoes, but it was a bad day for us. After that, we sold all the big ones and kept all the small ones. The only big potatoes we got were the ones that got nicked or cut when we plowed them out. We boiled the small ones and slid the peels off and then sliced them for frying. They were already cooked so they did not fry too well.

Potatoes were subject to attack by potato beetles. There were two kinds of beetles, hard-shelled striped ones and soft-shelled red ones. Either one would devastate a potato patch in a matter of days. Our solution to this problem was to sprinkle the potato plants with arsenate of lead to poison any bug that ate the leaves. We mixed the arsenate of lead with water in a milk bucket and used a small limb from a cedar tree as a sprinkler. Yes, we used the same milk bucket when we milked the cows. We would fill a bucket about half-full with the poisonous solution, dip the cedar branch in the solution, and sprinkle the potato plants as we walked along a row. In the process, our pants legs got completely soaked with the solution as did our hands. Today, we go bananas about a trace amount of arsenic in our drinking water and about the small amount of lead in wall paint. When I was a kid we got wet with a compound of both of these "hazardous" materials and we are still here over 70 years later. Go figure!

Canning Fruit

BESIDES THE VEGETABLES IN THE GARDEN, we also raised various fruits. A major crop was grapes. When I was a child, we had only purple grapes which grew in big clusters. When they were ripe, we would pick them and wash them, sorting out and throwing away the decayed and unripe small ones. Sometimes the small unripe ones were set aside to be made into jelly. The others were squeezed between two fingers which forced the center part containing the seeds out of the purple peel. The center pulp was placed in a colander and forced through the holes, leaving the seeds behind. The seedless pulp was then cooked and canned with the peels. We usually used the canned grapes in a pudding mixture as a dessert at supper (dinner to you city dudes). Canned grapes had a characteristic that I thoroughly disliked. After being in the can for a long time, they would form small flat crystals which could not be chewed. That always made me think that the grapes were contaminated somehow.

We also had peaches of a number of varieties. In early days we had trees which produced large peaches, mostly freestones, which we sliced and canned with sugar. They were good eaten straight out of the can or made into pies. As time went by, these peach trees died and were not replaced. I remember one peach tree, in its dying gasps, produced only two peaches which were gigantic. They were at least four inches in diameter. We saved the seeds but I don't believe we ever planted them. That tree never produced another peach.

We had another variety of peach which was small. These peaches were strange! One tree produced only green peaches that had loads of freckles and were freestones. Another produced only green peaches that were clingstone but did not have the freckles. Actually, the peaches weren't totally green when ripe. They did get a faint tinge of white to them. Another produced freestones that got only a blush of pink when they were ripe. We canned these in various ways. The freestones were cut in halves and canned, sometimes with the peelings and sometimes not. We peeled the clingstones and canned them whole with a sweet clove spice. The freestones with peelings usually wound up in a pudding as dessert. The clingstones were eaten off the seeds as a desert. For some strange reason we called all these varieties October peaches.

When I was a kid, we did not have any apple trees so we did not can apples ordinarily. Once in a while Dad would buy a bushel in town and we would can them, but this did not happen too often.

Cherries also were a fruit that we canned. In the early years we had two kinds of cherries, red ones that grew on a tree east of the smoke house (later, one on the barn lot side of the fence near the brooder house) and two black cherry trees just east of the hen house. The trees grew rather tall, so picking the cherries involved us kids climbing into the tree to pick most of them and Dad or one of us standing on something to pick the rest. We never had a step-ladder to use. Once, Dad broke a rib when he stood on a high chair to pick some of them and tipped over. After they were picked, they had to be pitted (removing the stones). This was not a fun job. We used bobby pins to dig the pit out of each cherry. Squeezing them like grapes would not work. They were canned with sugar and most often wound up in pies.

We canned sweet potatoes, but I don't know whether to call them fruits or vegetables.

One staple fruit we always canned was wild blackberries. There were a number of blackberry patches on neighboring farms that we had access to. For some reason, we had hardly any blackberry patches on our place. We kids would take a number of two-and-one-half gallon milk buckets up the road to Siebeneck's or Uncle Frank's farm and pick until they were full. They were very heavy to carry the mile or so back home. The berries were washed and canned whole. We would can up to 200 quarts of them so it took many milk buckets full. In the winter we would eat them as an additive to a pudding or as a substitute for syrup on sour milk pancakes. A blackberry patch was a good place to get scratched by briars, bitten by many chiggers, or get scared by the occasional snake.

We also picked wild raspberries (which were scarce) and wild gooseberries (which were small). These usually wound up in jellies. When I was young we did not raise any strawberries so we never had any strawberry jam.

Hair

DAD HAD A PAIR OF HAND CLIPPERS which he used to cut our hair. But someone had to cut Dad's hair and the job fell to me. I did not like to do it for two reasons. First, it was tough to get the hair even because the clippers had to be powered by hand and the hand got tired and unsteady. Secondly, as I've already mentioned, one's hand got extremely tired.

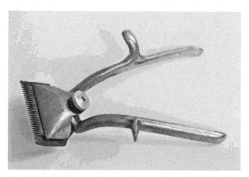

Hand-Operated Hair Clippers

During the 1930s, money was scarce so hardly anyone drove to town and, if they did, then haircuts there cost real money. So Dad became somewhat of a community barber, doing haircuts on Saturday evenings for free. If he had charged a nickel, it would have bought us a lot of candy. He did it in the living room and the men sat around in chairs shooting the breeze while Dad did the work. My uncle Hugo once borrowed the clippers and it came back with the tip of one of the shears broken off. Dad asked him how it got that way and Uncle Hugo said that it just broke. Unfortunately for Hugo, his son Leonard piped up and said, "No Dad, that happened when you got mad and threw the clippers out the door." We never did get an electric clippers and I cut Dad's hair with the old hand-operated one until I left home.

Our sisters were not much better off. In the early days, there was no such thing as a home permanent and both of my sisters were blessed with naturally straight hair. They usually wore their hair in braids. My mother made us boys (me at least) do the braiding sometimes. I am sure my sisters did not look forward to that any more than

I did.

If they wanted their hair curly, they were doomed to using water and hair curlers overnight for a temporary set. Such a curl would last at most a day or two and would have to be done often. Another alternative was to use a hair curler. What we had was a curling iron that had to be heated in a kerosene lamp chimney. Just look at the picture below.

Curling Iron

Nowadays there is such a thing as an electric hair curler. Later, home permanents came in and I have a faint recollection of giving Mom one myself. I gave my wife home permanents in our early married years, but she finally called it quits because I was impossibly slow.

Grandpa and Grandma Veit

I WAS 14 when Grandpa Veit died so I got to know him fairly well. My Grandma Veit died 10 years later but I was away from home most of the time after Grandpa died so I didn't get to see much more of Grandma. When I was small, they lived three and a half miles up the road so I didn't get to see very much of them then. They owned a big 300 acre farm then which included bottom and hill land. They bought the farm in 1914 and moved there from Taos. They kept their Taos farm for quite a while and some of their children lived on it and farmed it.

Two of their sons, Frank and Otto, lived with them on the Osage Bend farm and helped with the farm work, which was quite labor intensive in those days. When they first moved to the Osage

Bend farm, Grandpa installed a woven wire fence between his land and the "Club Land" which lay to the east. As a boy, I was intrigued by the form of the woven wire which had triangular openings instead of the normal rectangular ones. My dad told me that the woven wire fence had been made on the spot. I often wondered how it was done. In June 2001, in a museum, I ran across the type of machine that made such woven wire. I took a picture of it and include it here although it does not show the equipment very well.

Woven Wire-Making Machine

When the gravel county road between Osage Bend and Osage Bluff was made into an all-weather road in 1937, all the gravel came from a gravel bar in the Osage River on Grandpa's farm. He charged a penny a load, provided the county would take out a 20-year's supply and stockpile it. That stockpile stood along Grandpa's private road for years before it was all used up.

The road was graded, and then four inches of river gravel was spread on it. The gravel, as it came out of the river, was not screened and contained some large rocks. It was spread on the road as it came. My grandfather and Emil Rackers used four-pronged rakes and raked all five miles of gravel to get out the big rocks.

Grandpa and Grandma sold their big farm to two of their sons, Frank and Otto, and bought one a mile from Osage Bend along the road. We then lived at the third house up the road from them. My Grandpa always kept his hay frame on the ground near the road under a big oak tree. When Mom was not watching, my sister Mary Ann and I would go down the road and play on the hay frame. I was five and Mary Ann was two. Mom would look for us and see us down there. She would yell, "Quentin, Mary Ann, get home!" It was close to a quarter mile, yet we could hear her. Mom had a great voice when she was younger. Mom never understood why Grandma didn't see us and send us home. I personally think that Grandma saw us and enjoyed watching us out of her window.

Later, in 1936, my parents bought Grandpa and Grandma's farm and they moved into the house just up the road from where they had been. There I watched Grandpa grow and cure tobacco for his own use. It was illegal to sell tobacco without first getting a license. Grandma had her big garden next to Grandpa's tobacco patch and cultivated it diligently.

My Grandpa also made wine. He squeezed the juice out of the grapes with a big press that had a round hopper into which the grapes were placed. A big hand-turned screw forced a circular lid, which fit into the hopper, down onto the grapes and pressed out the juice. The wine he made was semi-sweet. He always said that if it was not sweet enough one could always add sugar. One year I made some blackberry wine and didn't use much sugar. It was extremely dry and no one but my

Grandma would drink it.

Grape and Cider Press Like Grandpa Veit's

Grandpa always had a mason jar of Queen Anne's lace tea brewing on the wood stove. He would cut off the tops of the weed and steep them upside down in water. Supposedly Queen Anne's lace is poisonous, but it never killed him. Grandpa supplied the yeast for the homemade bread that his grown children and in-laws baked. Every week, I or a sibling would go up the road to Grandpa's and get a number of cakes of yeast. The cakes were made with cornmeal. Grandpa was also the source for kerosene and I remember once going up the road to get a gallon. The cap on the can was missing and I spilled some on my leg. I would never have thought it would happen, but it raised a blister on my leg about six inches long. Grandpa came from the old country and it was said that he and his brother Alois possessed strange powers. I know that my Grandpa could "witch" for water and did so for our first well. He also seemed protected from insect stings. I once saw Dad plow into a stump that contained a nest of yellow jackets which stung the horses and caused them to break the double tree on the plow. He walked back home and up the road to his dad's. Grandpa got a gallon of kerosene and walked with Dad back to the field. He walked right up to the stump and the yellow jackets swarmed all over him but seemed not to sting him. He pulled the plow away from the stump and poured the kerosene on the stump. He then lit the kerosene and it seemed to attract the yellow jackets which flew into the flames and died. End of the trouble.

Being seven years old when he left Germany,

Grandpa spoke High German fluently. Grandma was quite intelligent. She came from a Low German speaking family and naturally could speak the language, but she also was fluent in High German and subscribed to the "St. Joseph's Blatt," a High German newspaper. However, strangely, she could not sign her name. She got a pension check because her son was killed in World War I and she always brought it to Dad, who signed her name after she had made her "X".

Grandpa was a mild and far-thinking man. I heard this secondhand, but I believe it to be true. Grandpa was in his late seventies and was planting fruit trees. A neighbor came by and asked why he was doing that since he would never live to see the fruit. Grandpa just said that someone did it for him and it was his turn to do it for somebody else. He used "cuss" words sparingly. The worst of them was "Py Dammit" and "Hot Day." I heard him use both of these when his kids and grandkids were visiting him and one of the grandkids threw a football through his living room window.

Uncle Joe, Grandpa's oldest son, was killed in World War I fighting against Germany. This must have been extremely hard because Grandpa was born in Germany. Again, secondhand from Dad, Grandpa was approached to buy Liberty Bonds to support the war and said that he had already bought some and would buy no more. The bond seller implied that Grandpa was a German sympathizer. Grandpa said, "I have a son over there, I am as loyal as anybody," and ran the seller off with a shotgun.

Our siblings were born at home and we stayed at Grandpa and Grandma's while the births were taking place. We got to sleep on the Davenport (a word unused today) which unfolded into a bed. This of course was a great treat. Grandpa shaved with a straight razor, a folding contraption with a four-inch long blade. I always wondered why he didn't cut himself with it. He sharpened the razor by stroking it along a leather strap called a "razor strop" which hung on the wall. When we kids would get out of hand he would threaten to use the strop on us. That usually would quieten us down.

I remember when Grandma came down the road to get Dad to help his brother Otto, who was kicked in the head by a mule. My cousin Francis Veit was with Uncle Otto at the time and called

Grandma. We didn't have a telephone because Dad had given Grandpa and Grandma his. Dad hauled Uncle Otto to the hospital, where he died the next day. Uncle Otto had never married. I could tell many a story about Uncle Otto, but I don't have the time or space for more than one.

Uncle Otto was a bachelor and was a favorite with us kids. We often rode home with him from church and when we did, he usually would stop and talk with Dad for a while. One time he and Dad were talking by the old barn and noticed one of Uncle George Braun's roosters fluffing himself in the barn dirt. Uncle Otto remarked that he had read that chickens were frightened by the color red and wondered if that were true. He and Dad tried an experiment. They caught the rooster and Uncle Otto tied his red handkerchief around the rooster's wing and let it loose. It stood there for a moment, then looked around and saw the handkerchief. It moved forward and the handkerchief followed. This alarmed the rooster and he took out across the field toward his home at an unbelievable pace. We lost sight of him as he neared Uncle George's. Uncle Otto lost his handkerchief which had come off the rooster somewhere along the way. A few years later the story came out and Uncle George said that he had seen the rooster head into his garage just a-panting away and wondered why.

Grandma was a great church goer and walked the mile to church every morning until she was 80 years old. By the way, I baked her 80th birthday cake, a three-layered confection, and we put 80 candles on it. I believe it was the first birthday cake she ever had.

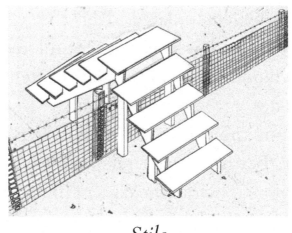

Stile

Grandma always liked spring water and would cross the road and a stile Dad had built for her over the hog pasture fence and get her daily bucket of water from the spring. We older boys teased our sisters, Mary Ann and Catherine, that they were born in the spring (March 17 and April

24) and it always got them riled up.

In her last years, Grandma lived with us and often sat in her rocking chair patching our overalls. She needed something else to do so Mom would let her help quilt. However, her eyesight had gotten bad and her stitches would be atrociously large. After Grandma had gone to bed, Mom would take the stitches out and do them over. Grandma never seemed to notice. She lived in our small upstairs bedroom and brought a dresser along with her for her use. It had a gummy black finish accumulated over the years. We refinished it and it was a beautiful red cherry wood. Grandma was impressed. I often wonder who got it.

Grandma moved up the road to live with her daughter, Bertha, for a while and broke her hip there. This was before the days of hip pins and the like and Grandma was bedridden the rest of her life. I visited with her there with my wife shortly before I graduated from college and went to Philadelphia. I was at Philadelphia when Grandma died in 1955 and did not see her again.

Christmas

AT LEAST A WEEK BEFORE CHRISTMAS, we would begin to bake cookies in the shape of Christmas trees, Santa Claus, and whatnot to be decorated with icing and hung on the Christmas tree. Our tree was always a cedar tree cut on the farm. We kids would go out with Dad to select the tree. It was brought home and set up in our parents' bedroom downstairs. Several days before Christmas, newspaper would appear, covering the windows in the bedroom, and the door would be locked. Our larger toys would also disappear.

On Christmas morning the newspaper would be gone and there would be the tree all decorated with toys under it. A number of the toys would be our old larger toys which sported a new coat of paint. It was during the Depression and I suppose our parents couldn't afford new big toys, but could afford the paint. The decorated tree would be covered with the cookies baked and decorated previously. Kids would sneak a cookie off the tree and rearrange the hangings so its disappearance wasn't noticeable.

Of course we went to Mass in the morning (there was no midnight Mass). Only at Christmas were the hymns sung in German, and I dearly loved hearing them, although I could translate hardly a word of them. Everyone wished everyone else a Merry Christmas. We kids could not wait to get back home and play with the toys.

I remember one Christmas at the old place when Rod and Clarence got brand new trucks with lights that really worked. That is, they worked until our cousin Francis Veit shot the bulbs out with a BB gun he had gotten for Christmas. I also remember a small windup toy my sister Mary Ann got for Christmas. She must have been about four years old. It ran around in crazy gyrations and would rear up and back up. She was always scared of it and we boys got a great kick out of winding it up and sending it towards her.

One of the problems with hanging cookies on the tree for decoration was mice. Mice would climb the tree and eat the back out of a cookie. The cookie would hang there with only the front icing. I never could understand why they did not eat the sweet icing instead of the cookie. No accounting for tastes! After the house was remodeled, the Christmas tree was always placed in the living room.

For us, Christmas time was also a time for visiting neighbors, when the adults often played cards. One year, while the Schmidts were visiting at the Hoelschers, their house burned to the ground. I was good friends with one of their sons, Jerry, (retired Doctor Schmidt now) and often visited with him in the house. It was a log house with a long upstairs room which Jerry used as his laboratory. We're talking grade school years here. Jerry had collected all the muzzle-loading guns, all the crystal radios, and all the other weird inventions that the people in Osage Bend had owned at one time or another. He made such things as hand-held fountain pen guns, molded lead bullets, electric cockroach killers, telegraphs, etc. All this was destroyed in the fire.

Meals

WE VEITS HAD FIVE MEALS A DAY in the summertime. We almost always had cooked oatmeal with milk for breakfast. I hated oatmeal in a number of ways. I had to get up in the morning and start the fire in the kitchen wood stove and cook a big pot of oatmeal while my older brothers helped Dad with the chores. Then came the eating and oatmeal was not a favorite with me. Then came the pot washing, but not always. Sometimes the pot washing came first because an oatmeal pot was hard to clean and, in the morning, might be surreptitiously slid under the kitchen cabinet to await me the next morning when it came time to cook some more.

Once in a while we had corn meal mush, which I thought was even worse than oatmeal. In later years we had puffed wheat which could be bought in a big sack for 16¢, the same price as a box of oatmeal. We had bacon for breakfast only on Sundays. For a short period of time after we had butchered hogs, it was fried-down bacon which had a much better taste than the salt-cured kind. Eggs were too precious to eat for breakfast, although they showed up once in a while as scrambled eggs for supper.

I loved lunch out in the field. Here coffee would be brought out in a mason jar. The coffee could not be poured directly into the jar because the sudden temperature change would break the jar. Instead, the milk (whole with 4% cream) would be put into the jar first and the coffee poured into it. This produced a taste completely different than ordinary coffee with cream. In ordinary coffee, the milk/cream is added to the hot coffee and the heat causes the cream to form into tiny invisible curds, giving the coffee a slightly bitter taste. In the cream-first process, the cream is heated up gradually and does not curdle, yielding (to my mind at least) a much better tasting coffee.

Potatoes were a staple for both the big meals, dinner and supper. Usually they were fried. When we sold potatoes, most of the big ones, except for those damaged at harvest, went to market and we had very few big potatoes to peel and fry. Instead, we kept the small ones and cooked them, peeled off the skins, sliced, and then fried them. They were not nearly as good as the big fried ones. We often ate the potatoes with milk gravy on top.

At noon in the summertime and on Saturdays we often had chicken, ham hock, or backbone soup with egg noodles. Mom made the noodles, and we sliced them. They had to be sliced very, very thin to please her. I believe one reason was that there would appear to be more noodles that way.

The lunch we took to school consisted of homemade bread smeared with a mixture of peanut butter and molasses or jelly. Rich kids occasionally had a boiled egg, orange, or banana. I envied them.

In the evening, we often had what we called milk soup. It was really a thin vanilla pudding, which we ladled over homemade bread. When enough hard crusts and slices of the homemade bread collected, we would have a skillet of bread pudding. It was always made in a skillet. The bread would be broken up into the skillet and a small amount of hot water poured over the bread to soften it and then an egg and milk mixture would be poured over that. The mixture was cooked in the skillet on top of the stove.

Sour-milk pancakes were a staple also. We didn't have refrigeration and the pot of milk we kept out for use in the house would often spoil by evening. Sour-milk pancakes were easy, a pot of sour milk, a spoonful of baking soda, an egg, flour, and a little salt. Stirred up, it was ready to be fried in the skillet. For syrup, we usually used canned blackberries and sugar.

For company dinner on Sunday, we mostly had fried chicken and a number of vegetables. The chicken was killed and dressed that same day. For dessert, we would have cake and pie. At one time I could have mixed up a yellow cake from scratch and baked it with my eyes blindfolded. I wasn't too good at pies.

Happenings up the Road

WHEN I WAS BORN, we lived up the road about a half-mile. We moved down the road in August of the year I turned five. So I don't remember a whole lot about that time, but I do remember some.

I remember my brothers Clarence and Rod getting toy trucks for Christmas that had lights that really worked. That is, they worked until cousin Francis Veit shot them out with a BB gun he had got for Christmas.

I've told about the pitcher pump we had up there. Another thing we had that we kids used as a play thing was the wagon seat with springs. It was made to fit on a box wagon and softened the ride somewhat on steel wheel wagons. It stood on the concrete in the small room attached to our garage and we kids used it as a sofa. I never saw it on a wagon and I believe it must have been left when we moved down the road because I don't remember ever seeing it down there.

Spring Wagon Seat

We milked cows and separated the milk and cream. I don't know whether we sold any of the cream or not. I do know that we churned butter from some of it because I was blamed for breaking the butter churn which always stood in the front (living) room (which we never used). I can remember the cream running across the floor. If I got a licking for it, I just don't recall.

We had a hand-cranked DeLaval cream separator that was painted red. The milk was poured into a big bowl at the top. The crank was then turned, and turned, and turned, and turned, until the large fly-wheel got up to speed. When it was up to speed the thing really hummed. While it was being cranked up to speed a little bell would ring with every revolution of the crank. When the crank was going fast enough, centrifugal force held the bell ball bearing in place and the bell would quit ringing.

Cream Separator

What was being cranked was a stack of cone-shaped discs which acted as a centrifuge. When it was up to speed a spigot on the bowl would be opened, allowing the unseparated milk to enter the top center of the centrifuge. The heavier milk would be spun down toward the bottom and the lighter cream would float to the top. The skimmed milk would flow out of a lower spout and was ultimately fed to the pigs. The lighter cream would flow out of a top spout and would be saved. We had the cream separator after we moved down the road and used it until we began to sell bulk milk. It stood out in the smoke house. I don't know when Dad got rid of it. I saw one almost like it in a museum and took a picture which I include here.

There was a brush patch across the road which made a great play area and we used it a lot. There was an old road, just across the county road, that led down to Adrian's and ultimately to the lower road. We would go on this road about a quarter mile to the top of the hill where one could look down on Adrian's. There stood Grandpa Veit's old horse-powered baler which we played in. To my knowledge, we never went down to Adrian's. The Adrian boys would come to visit us, however. I think there were five of them but I don't remember all their names. I do know there were Mike and Ed. Mike wore a full beard and when my sister Mary Ann would see him she would start screaming. She had to be taken into another room.We had two cow pastures, the upper and lower. The upper pasture was surrounded by woven wire and we kept pigs in it too. There was a wooden stile between the two that the cows could step over, but a pig could not. There was a dug out and walled-in spring with a pump at the lower end of the upper pasture. We could move the pump aside and climb down into the spring. It was about four feet down into the spring. This adventure came to a screeching halt when we climbed into it once and found we had a snake for company.

The cows always seemed to wind up in the lower pasture when it was time to bring them in for milking. We boys would then have to go get them. I don't remember doing this much except for one time. Then we went to get the cows and they were at the top of the hill towards Braun's in the back pasture. It also was thundering and lightning. We started the cows running down the hill and each grabbed a cow's tail and hung on.

You could not run as fast as the cows so you just jumped into the air every so often. Our feet would hit the ground about every six feet or so.

One time, Rod and Clarence went to get the cows and came home with a strange man with a gun following them. Of course they were frightened. It seems the man had been out hunting with a group from the "Club House" (I think) and got lost. When he came upon the boys he knew they would lead him back to "civilization." He had to wait until Dad finished milking and then Dad took him back to where he belonged. I rode along with Dad in the car. It was dark by then and I was impressed by all the lanterns carried by people who were looking for him.

When Dad and Mom went to town (Jefferson City) they often left us boys in the care of a baby sitter, Gladys Weckenborg, daughter of Mom's good friend of Osage Bluff, the blacksmith's wife. Gladys was only about 14 and a "hell on wheels." One time we boys climbed up into the barn hayloft and looked out the big door used to put hay in the loft. Gladys stood below and told Clarence Jr. that she would catch him if he jumped. He did, and Gladys, of course, just stepped back and let him hit the ground. He survived, and we all thought it was great fun and jumped out many times afterward. It was not that small of a jump and I often wonder why we didn't break a leg. I have a crippled foot where two bones are fused together. I've been told by doctors that it was a birth defect, but I wonder if this jumping might have caused it.

One time Gladys set one of the flues (chimneys) on fire by overloading the stove. The stove got red hot. Dad came home in time to climb on the roof and throw salt down the chimney.

Gladys got us boys in trouble one time by having us haul her down the road on the corn cultivator. We were her horses. Well, we lost control and she and the cultivator wound up in the ditch. We had a hard time explaining to Dad how the cultivator got in the ditch alongside the road. I could tell other incidents about Gladys, but will refrain from doing so to protect the sensibilities of the reader.

I've been told that I had "wanderlust" and would often run away from home. I told about going down to Grandma Veit's house. I apparently also followed the mailman and wagon drivers up the road although I have no memory of it. I've been told that I was found at least a mile and a half from home. I've already told about knocking the leg from a table and breaking a lot of dishes.

My mother, like most farm women then, canned most of our winter food. We kept this in a cellar beneath the house. Of course, this was in the days before electricity and there was no light in the cellar. If we didn't want to light a lantern and take it with us, we would just leave the cellar door at the top of the stairs open to give a little light and feel for the jars we wanted. We memorized where everything was stored on the shelves. This had almost disastrous consequences one time when Mary Ann, who was still getting around in a baby walker with wheels, pedaled herself to the top and then down the stairs into the stone wall at the bottom. After that somebody watched her when we went down to the cellar.

One time, one of my brothers feeling in the dark, picked up a glass jar and brought it up, only to find a small snake wrapped around the top.

Strange as it may seem, I don't remember a single toy I got for Christmas when we lived up the road. Maybe I didn't get any! It's funny, the things one remembers and what one forgets. I can remember Clarence and Rod walking down the road toward school with wool socks over their shoes so they could walk on the slick ice that covered everything. This I remember and I bet they both don't.

Wintertime

WINTER HAD ITS SPECIAL TIMES. One thing we kids longed for was deep snow. When it came there was no such thing as a "snow day" as modern school kids have. We still had school and we still walked our mile to school. Uncle Frank lived up the road three and one-half miles from the school and he had two kids in school when I was there. When the snow was deep, he hooked a team of horses up to a homemade, triangular-shaped snow plow. He drove this contraption down the road pushing the snow to both sides. As he went by, the kids along the way would fall in behind the plow and walk as a group. This was a fun time.

Also, when it snowed, it was time for sled riding behind the barn. We had a great hill there, at least two tenths of a mile long. We would tramp a curving track down the hill and away we would go. We had a "Flyer" sled which we got for Christmas one time. We had it a week when Dad broke a part out of one of the long top pieces, hauling the cast iron kettle. The piece never got fixed and we used the sled with the piece broken out.

The Braun kids would join us going down the hill. I felt sorry for them because they only had a wooden sled with two-by-four runners that Uncle George had made. It did not go down the hill nearly as well as our steel runner sled. If Uncle George had only thought about it a bit, he would have planed the runners in a "V" shape and it would have slid much better.

The more we used the track, the icier it got and the sled would attain a great speed. We built a small "ski jump" near the bottom of the hill and it was thrilling to go over it at high speed. It was the downfall of the sled though. One time, my brother Clarence and our cousin Francis Veit went down the hill, hit the "ski jump" and the sled just collapsed from the shock of the impact and their combined weight. End of sled.

Wintertime had its other pleasures. Huckleberries (hackberries) were ripe and there was a good patch on Ted Rackers' property near the east end of our farm. These were ripe in late fall and early winter and we picked them by the handful and ate them, that is, we ate the outer shell. The berries were about the size of a BB and the outer shell was about a 64th of an inch thick. There was no content to them since the inner part was hard wood and we spit that out, but they had a good flavor. There was another winter fruit and that was black haws. They grew on trees across the road, in clusters somewhat like grapes, and were about one-half inch long. They were purplish-black in color and tasted a little like plums. They stayed on the trees well into the winter.

Spoon and Knife Shapes inside Persimmon

Another wild fruit, good to eat, was persimmons. These were orange-ish in color and had a number of flat seeds. Some people picked them and made jelly out of them. We didn't. A flat seed, when split open, revealed a knife and spoon hidden inside. One had to be careful that the persimmons were ripe before eaten. An unripe persimmon was very astringent and puckered up the mouth something awful.

Another thing that winter brought was the ability to make homemade ice cream. Our watering trough was fashioned out of concrete and was shaped to withstand the hardest freeze. It was a source of ice for making ice cream in the winter. When we could talk Mom into it, she would make the custard necessary for the ice cream and it would be up to us kids to get it frozen. We packed cracked ice from the water trough around a gallon bucket set into a two and one-half gallon milk bucket. We added salt to the ice and proceeded to rotate the bucket back and forth by grasping its handle. This was very hard on the wrists and could not be done very long. So each kid took turns twisting the handle back and forth. Salt has a peculiar effect on ice. It causes ice to melt and, in the process of melting, the ice absorbs a tremendous amount of heat. An ice, salt, and water mix will reach temperatures below zero degrees Fahrenheit. It still took quite a while for the ice cream to freeze, but the taste was worth it.

Another thing that occurred during winter was the coming of the snow birds. These were small, plump little birds with white breasts. Normally, they could not be caught, but if a deep snow happened, they would burrow into it and one could sneak up on them and trap one in a burrow. We would catch them and let them go. One time though, I caught one and took it inside. For some reason, we had a fire in the heating stove in the living room. I guess it was unusually cold. Anyhow someone opened the heating stove door and the bird flew right out of my hand directly into the fire and was instantly incinerated.

We had single-pane windows without any storm windows, so whenever it got cold the windows frosted up. We wrote our names in the frost with our warm fingers. In extreme cold weather, the frost would not melt. Instead, the ice would turn clear and this worked just as well. Of course, on cold nights the water bucket would freeze up in the kitchen and any water sneaked upstairs in a fruit jar would freeze and break the jar. The house was clapboard on the outside over oak siding that had large cracks between the boards. There was no insulation between the studs. It was plastered on the inside but the plaster stopped at the top of the baseboard. On snowy days, the snow would seep through cracks between the outside boards and under the baseboard and leave a coating of snow on the floor.

We kids slept upstairs with no heat. It was often cold as the devil. We slept under what we called feather beds. These were as wide as the beds and made of striped ticking filled with chicken or goose feathers. They were cold as ice when you first got under them, but they soon warmed up and were toasty warm. When winter came we changed to long johns for underwear. These were woolen and buttoned down the front and had a button-up back flap for trips to the outdoor privy. After sleeping all night, the trip to the privy was often made barefooted, even through the snow. When nature calls everyone answers. We wore the long johns all the time and changed them once a week when they got washed. We went without them that day because we only had one pair. I wonder why we called them a pair when they were one piece outfits.

COMMUNITY

Church Customs

OUR SEATING CUSTOM at St. Margaret Church in Osage Bend was for men to sit on the right and women to sit on the left. Children sat in the front pews. Each organization within the parish was assigned one Sunday of the month on which their members would sit together in a reserved part of the church and receive Holy Communion as a body. The area reserved for the organization's Communion Sunday was denoted by a banner attached to the end of a pew in the center aisle. As they entered the church, the sodality members were given badges to wear. These were returned after Mass. At the 2001 Veit Reunion at Osage Bend, Missouri, the local deacon read my draft of this appendix and remarked that he had just found the badges and had wondered what they were for.

Now he knew.

The sanctuary was separated from the congregation by the Communion rail, a railing with gates at the center aisle. A cloth held in place by rods hung on the sanctuary side. At Communion time, this cloth was lifted and laid over top of the rail. The Communicants knelt at the railing when they received Communion and an altar boy held a gold plate under the Communicant's chin to catch any crumbs that might fall off the Host. The recipient had to fast from the previous midnight and I believe this included water.

There were no readings by the laity, nor any petitions. There was an epistle (no second reading), a first gospel, and a last gospel. Everything was in Latin, except for the sermon which, by the time I was old enough to remember, was in English instead of German.

The priest and acolytes faced the altar away from the people during Mass. There were three picture frames set up on the altar, a small one on the left, a large one in the middle, and a small one on the right. I don't remember what the first frame held (I believe it was the Offertory Prayers), but the middle one had what is today the first Eucharistic Prayer (the Canon then) in Latin and the one on the right had the Last Gospel (the beginning of the Gospel according to John) in Latin. When Mass was over these frames were placed face down on the altar and the whole covered with another altar cloth. The Epistle and Gospel book was held on a stand which was moved by the acolyte from one side of the altar to the other. For the Epistle reading it was on the left and for the Gospel reading it was on the right.

There were two types of Masses: High Mass and Low Mass. At High Mass the Gloria, Credo, Sanctus and Pater Noster were sung by the choir. The priest chanted the Canon and the lead-in to the Gloria, Credo, Santus and Pater Noster. The priest wore black vestments for funerals. I don't believe there are any black vestments today. The acolytes wore black cassocks and white surplices for most Masses including High Masses for funerals and red cassocks and white surplices for regular High Mass. There were prayers after Mass for the conversion of Russia.

There were Ember Days, on a Wednesday, Friday, or Saturday following the first Sunday in

Lent, Pentecost, September 14, and December 13.
These were days of fast and abstinence. There
were Rogation Days on the three days before
Ascension and on April 25. These were days of
prayer for the harvest. We also had a Corpus
Christi Procession in which the Blessed Sacrament
was carried from altar to altar under a canopy.

*Canopy Held Over Priest at Outdoor Mass. My
Uncle Rudolph Veit at Left*

The choir was up in a loft at the rear of the
church. The organ was a reed type and someone
had to pump the bellows by hand during services.

In the early days of Osage Bend, the church was heated by stoves with pipes running 20 or more feet up to the ceiling. Later, a space was excavated under the center of the church and a wood furnace, with a grate as wide as the center aisle atop it, was installed. It got awfully hot if one happened to stop on the grate during a procession.

Old Osage Bend Church

The original church was huge, with the outside

studs being oak two-by-twelves, 24 feet long. The windows were high enough off the floor so that one was not tempted to look out during services. Before electricity, the church was illuminated by kerosene lamps which were mounted on brackets on the walls and the roof supporting posts.

Typical Church Lamp

The kneelers were plain wood with no padding. They were not attached to the pews, and scooted around and turned over easily, causing many a kid to get grief from a parent after church. The sanctuary lamp hung by a counterbalanced chain from the ceiling at the center of the sanctuary. The three altars were very ornate and were handmade by one of the early parishioners, Anton Bode (maybe with help from his brothers). When the new church was built, the old altars were burned in the lot across from his house. A few of the old pews are still used on the grounds at picnic time. My Veit grandparents donated the large crib (creche) set used at Christmas time in the old church. It was at least six by ten feet and was too big for the new church. I don't know what happened to it. The church steeple was quite tall, probably 50 feet high. My dad always painted the roof on it. He would get on the peak of the roof, throw a rope over the cross, and dangle by the rope while he painted. The bell hung in the steeple with two ropes hanging down just inside the church entrance. One rope rang the bell regularly and one tolled the bell for funerals. If a server put his heart into ringing the bell he could hang onto the rope and be drawn quite a ways up toward the ceiling. Too vigorous ringing and the bell actually tipped over and someone would have to climb to the belfry to right it. For tolling, the rope was pulled and then let go for each toll. This drew back a hammer, which when let go, would hit against the outer side of the bell. The bell, without the toller, is still used now, mounted on the roof of the new church.

From the time I could first remember we had a "grouchy" old priest, Father Wagoner. He had two adopted daughters who lived with him in the rectory. I remember one of them was named Connie. Father Wagoner generated enough discord in the parish that most of the families would not allow their boys to serve as acolytes. For a while it was just the Veit and Hoelscher boys along with Albert Renterghem. Sometime in the 1940s, Father Wagoner was retired to St. Mary's Hospital and an administrator, Father Oligschlager, came to us from St. Peters in Jefferson City. He had a basement put under the two-story rectory, a big cistern added, and a stone garage built by my dad. The garage was fancy. It had a stone in a heart shape embedded in the front stone wall. My brother Clarence and I went to see it at the Veit reunion in June 2001. Father Wagoner had a 1914 Gardner automobile in the old garage (which was torn down) and this was pulled away into the woods to rot. When we served Mass on weekdays, Albert Renterghem and I played in it a lot.

The parish had a DC electric power plant in a shed near the parish hall. This was used only at parish picnic time and furnished no power to the church. When Father Oligschlager arrived, the annual parish picnic (which had ceased under Father Wagoner) was revived. Father Oligschlager raised two steers on the church grounds that were butchered for the picnic. That's why he needed our fence posts.

As an afterthought I add that the outside of the church was tin, molded in the form of bricks, the store across the road was covered in tin in the form of stone, the one-room school house was covered in tin, and so was the Otto Hofer house a tenth of a mile away. This led to Osage Bend at one time being known as "Tin Town."

New Year

ON NEW YEAR'S EVE AT OSAGE BEND, men would gather and go from house to house, shooting fireworks and making a lot of noise. The resident was then expected to hand out a treat of some kind, usually in the form of food, such as sausage, bread, wine, or fruit. After making the rounds, the men would build a fire on a gravel bar at the creek, cook the food, and have a feast. Reading old German Newspapers from Jefferson City, I can trace the custom back at least to the 1870s.

The last time I went New Year's Shooting was around 1950 when I was back home from college. That time we used two log splitting guns. These were heavy steel "shell casings" with about one-half inch thick walls, a one and a half inch center

bore, and a fuse hole near the rear end. These
normally were filled with black powder and
driven into the end of a log and set off with a fuse
in the small hole. The resulting explosion split the
log.

Log-Splitting Gun

For New Year's Shooting, we filled the guns
three-quarters of the way with black powder and
hammered a wad of newspaper on top of that with
a sledge hammer and a big bolt. At Emmet
Wolters' house, we set two of these off under their
bedroom window. After the explosion, I heard

glass tinkling. The concussion had broken the window. We did not tell them and they wined and dined us. Later, when they returned to bed they found the room exceedingly cold and found the broken window. It was 10 degrees outside that night.

During that night everyone but Frank Braun and me overindulged, and he and I hauled the participants back home one by one. One cause was a wine drinking contest at Joe Bisges' place. Joe brought the wine up from his cellar by the pitcherful. I got home on New Year's morning in time to change clothes and start the milking. New Year was a Holy Day of Obligation, and I must confess that I felt like hell at Mass.

Visiting

SUNDAY AFTERNOONS were usually spent either visiting or being visited. I don't know how the arrangements were made, but almost every Sunday, except in winter, we were either visiting or being visited by aunts and uncles and their children. It was a fantastic treat when we visited someone like Uncle Carl and Aunt Esther Mertens or Ed and Louise Imhoff who lived 50 miles away at Tipton, Missouri. Of course we didn't get there alone. Other aunts and uncles would visit them the same day also. On one time that sticks in my memory, we stopped by Uncle Emil and Aunt Catherine's first and had an assortment of kids in the two cars as we went on to Uncle Carl's. I know that I was in the back seat of Uncle Emil's car at the driver side rear window as we sped up

Highway 50 to Tipton. Uncle Emil pushed his old (probably fairly new then) car up to 85 miles an hour. A hand stuck out the window would want to take off like an airplane.

The menfolk would usually play horseshoes, in a sort of tournament. My dad could throw ringers almost at will and it was not unusual to see four shoes around the stake at the same time. Uncle Ed Imhoff was blind in one eye and I often wondered how he could see well enough to pitch horseshoes, but he was good. The cousins would play touch football, with an occasional time out for a female cousin to change the diaper on one of her younger siblings. All the kids were outside. The women would "ka-snobble" in the house, exchanging the latest gossip, recipes, and whatnot. I often got stuck with cooking the chicken and baking the cake because my mother was bothered with heart problems then.

In the evening, the old folks would play pinochle in hard fought games with much slamming of fists on our poor dining room table. We kids would play outside in the dark, playing such games as "I brought back what I borrowed," or exchanging ghost stories, or some other such nonsense. One aunt and uncle lived across Turkey Creek in Callaway County and would stay overnight with us if we happened to have a heavy rain. Of course, Dad and we boys would have to take a timeout to do the chores in the evening, but that usually didn't take too long. Because of having cows to milk, we also could not stay too late when we visited elsewhere.

There is one visit that sticks in my mind. This was one by some Huhmann relatives from Chicago. I remember there were two boys, probably still of grade school age. They pestered to get to ride a horse and Dad finally put them on old Queen, who was a pretty red horse. We had no saddle so the two boys were on the horse bareback. The front one began to lose his balance and pulled on old Queen's opposite rein to try to right himself. Unfortunately, this made Queen circle in such a way as to make the boy fall more. Before Dad could grab Queen's head to stop her, both boys fell off and Queen stepped on the leg of one. It didn't break, but the black and blue mark left by Queen's steel shoe was obvious.

The Games Children Played

ANDY OVER WAS A FAVORITE CHILDREN'S GAME at family get-togethers. The equipment consisted of a ball and a building. The object of the game was to "capture" the members of the other team. The teams would take positions on opposite sides of the building. Someone on one of the teams would throw the ball over the house while shouting "Andy Over!" If the ball was not thrown hard enough to make it over the house, the thrower would shout "Back Ball!" and try again. If the ball did make it to the other side, someone on the opposing team had to catch it without a bounce (on the honor system).

If the ball was caught, the catcher would run around to the other side of the house and throw the ball at one of the opposing players, all of whom tried to escape to the opposite side without being hit. A player that was hit was thus "captured" and became a member of the capturing team. The team that had just received the ball would then would become the thrower. The game continued until all of the players were on one side. But if the ball was not caught, no run-around happened, and the team that had failed to catch the ball would then throw.

My wife remembers playing another game as a kid. It called for naming objects within view until one of the players could think of no visible object that had not already been mentioned. In ritual fashion, one person in the group would start the game by announcing "Ah!" The second would respond with "Bah!" Then came "Nah!" Then the naming of objects began. If one of the players could not think of another object to name, he was obliged to say "peewee." This would end the game, and the "peewee" was declared the loser.

At home, when company came, we played touch football sometimes and "I brought back what I borrowed." In "I brought back what I borrowed," one player whispered into each player's ear what they had borrowed, each thing being different. Another player whispered into each ear the reason the article was returned. Then each player in turn told out loud what they had borrowed and why they had returned it. Many of the combinations were hilarious. Nobody won, but we enjoyed the game.

Neighborhood Cooperatives

TWO ANNUAL CHORES demanded crews of more men than the average family had at their disposal: threshing and wood-sawing. For these chores, neighbors would get together and pool their manpower to get the job done.

In Osage Bend, we used the cooperative system for threshing wheat, oats, and barley. Steam engines went out of business at Osage Bend around 1930 and the thresher owners, the Hoelschers and the Renterghems, got big McCormick Deering tractors to power the machines. Hoelschers had two machines and two tractors, one set being quite a bit smaller than the other and it was the first they owned. In my time, it was kept in a shed and used only in emergencies when the bigger rig was down for repairs. Louis

Hoelscher gave the newest machine a good going over in the spring before threshing started and in my memory the machine broke down only once, at which time the smaller machine was called on.

Threshing Machine

Both tractors originally had steel wheels with lugs, but the steel rims were later cut off the larger tractor and rims welded on and rubber tires employed. The old threshing machine had steel wheels and the new machine had solid rubber tires. With the rubber tires, the machine wasted little time moving from one place to another. When the machine arrived at a place, it was carefully located and holes dug to level the machine. The machine, unlike today's combines, had to be level to operate properly. I suspect they would not have had to be perfectly level but nearly so. The chain conveyor which fed the bundles of grain into the machine was unfolded, the blower through which the straw exited was positioned, the grain conveyor tube was pointed to the side, the tractor was positioned with the belt around its pulley and that of the machine, and we were finally ready to go. Of course, before threshing could begin, the wheat had to be cut. We did this with a horse-drawn binder that had a six-foot platform (six-foot sickle, cutting a six-foot swath). The binder had a big rotating reel just ahead of the platform that pushed the wheat toward the sickle. As the sickle cut the wheat, it fell onto the platform canvas which rotated on two wood rollers. The rotating canvas took the cut wheat to two upward-slanting rotating canvases, one above the other, which delivered the wheat to the bundle tier. The canvases had spaced wood slats which caught the wheat and moved it along.

The bundle tier was a clever contraption that wrapped a binder twine around a bundle and tied it in a knot. The finished bundle was kicked out of the machine onto a bundle carrier attached to the side of the binder. When the bundle carrier was full, it was "tripped" and dumped its load of bundles. These were dumped in rows across the field and the bundles were shocked, ten to a shock, and one bundle was bent and spread out to form a cap for the shock. This work was done in June.

The binder was too wide to go through a gate or over most roads, so it was "trucked" for moving. The tongue was unhooked from the binder front and fastened to the end of the platform so the binder could be pulled longways. Two trucking wheels were attached to the front and back of the binder and the "bull" wheel, which furnished the drive power to the binder was cranked up and out of the way.

When the binder was pulled into a field, we first cut a big patch of wheat by hand using a cradle. A cradle was a scythe with attached fingers to catch the wheat as it was cut. The cut wheat was tied into bundles using strands of wheat for tying. Also, on the first round around a field the bull wheel mashed down a swatch of wheat. It was a job for us kids to take a stick and raise the wheat back up so it would not be missed when a "back round" was made to cut it.

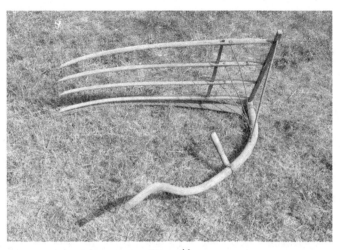

Cradle

A threshing crew consisted of the following: six men with teams and wagons; three or four bundle pitchers to toss the bundles onto the wagons; a blower tender; a tractor operator; one or two straw pile workers; three or four grain carriers (if the grain was not fed directly into a bin or truck); a machine operator; and perhaps two relief bundle pitchers to feed the machine. The crew was usually around 20 men. Young boys carried water in jugs out to the fields for the bundle pitchers and wagon drivers. There were no cups and everyone drank out of the same jug.

One year I made the mistake of agreeing to drive Louis Hoelscher's team when we threshed at his place. We always started on the 4th of July at his place because he was one of the machine owners and the machine was stored at his place. Other owners must have liked what they saw and I had to drive every owner's team that year, except for the six places where we furnished a team and I had to drive ours then. I guess it could have been worse. I could have been carrying 120 pound sacks of grain all day.

Hand-Operated Water Pump

The summer that I was 13 years old I worked for my uncle, Rudolph Veit. There, a steam engine was still in use for threshing and I got stuck with pumping the water for it by hand out of Sugar Creek in Miller County. That machine used 1500 gallons of water a day. It was a much bigger threshing machine than the one we had at Osage Bend. To pump the water, I used a hand-operated pump such as the one shown above. It had two-inch diameter intake and out-flow hoses. One stood at the pump and pushed the long handle back and forth. It was not so easy as it might look because one was raising a two-inch diameter stream of water up to 20 feet. Dad had one like it, but someone borrowed and never returned it. Dad never could bring himself to ask for something back and we lost many tools that way. One thing that was borrowed by a neighbor was a grain gleaning machine. It stood in his barn for years and I guess went to his kids or on his estate sale.

When it came to sawing wood, my uncle George Braun owned the saw rig. At first it was pulled by horses, and later by a Fordson tractor. It had its own single cylinder engine which would occasionally flood and refuse to start. Uncle George would unscrew the spark plug and hold a lit match to the hole. There would be a big "woosh" and he would screw the plug back in. It generally started after that. Other than for grain threshing, we usually traded help only with Uncle

George's family.

One time when we were sawing wood at Uncle George's place, the saw hit a metal object in the wood. The object turned out to be an old horseshoe. While Uncle George was filing the saw to re-sharpen it, he and Dad speculated about how the shoe got in the wood. Dad asked George where he had cut the wood and George told him that it was in such-and-such "holler."

"Why," Dad said, "we had a still in that 'holler' and we nailed a horseshoe up in a tree to hang the lantern on. I bet this is the same horseshoe."

Once in a while we would shred corn and this required more men than we had. In corn shredding, the corn stalks are fed into the threshing machine similar to, or the same as, the one used for threshing wheat. The corn is hauled from the field and fed into the machine. The output is ground up corn stalks and shelled grain.

Limestone Quarries

DAD WAS SOMEWHAT OF A PIONEER when it came to limestone. I helped Dad get together a pile of limestone that he intended to have crushed and spread on his fields. Back then, mobile lime crushers were brought to farms to do the job. For some reason, the crusher never showed up and the pile of limestone still lays there in the cow pasture across the road. I would imagine that someone coming upon it would wonder how and why it got there.

School

WHEN I STARTED ELEMENTARY SCHOOL (we called it grade school,) the school had only one room, and one teacher taught all eight grades. The school was heated by a wood-burning stove and our water came from a cistern which collected water from the roof. I remember only one time that the cistern was cleaned out. There was a load of black dirt where the water was dumped. We never thought twice about drinking the water.

We had two outdoor privies, one for the girls and one for the boys. The boy's had a tin urinal. A sidewalk led beside the cistern, straight downhill to the girl's privy and a sidewalk angled off that to the boy's privy. In the wintertime, when it was cold enough, some boys would get to school early and pump water from the cistern and pour it on the sidewalks and they would become a sheet of ice. This was a "no-no" of course, but still got done anyway. At noon time we would take a run at the top of the hill and skate on our shoe soles (no skates of course) down the sidewalk and bang into the door of the girl's privy. No girl dared to use the privy at lunch time.

The community was almost entirely Catholic. In my early years at school, a boy would go up to the church (a half-block up the road) at noon and ring the Angelus, which we all prayed. Then, before eating lunch we washed our hands. This was a regimented affair. We held our hands over a wash basin and one child poured water over our hands. We then soaped our hands from a dispenser mounted on the wall and moved on to the next spot where we held our hands over another basin as another kid poured water over our hands to rinse the soap off. A third kid handed us a paper towel to dry our hands.

After this ritual we then sat down to open our lunch boxes, which in my case consisted of a one-half gallon syrup pail containing two peanut butter and molasses bread sandwiches. My one male classmate would have a baloney or other lunch meat sandwich, a boiled egg, and an orange or banana. It was tough watching him eat. In later years, I understood the situation. He was the last of the Renterghem's kids, and the others were gone from home. The Renterghems owned a sawmill and threshing machine and could afford a nice lunch for their remaining kid.

We had a recess in the morning and afternoon plus the lunchtime break. In the fall and spring we played anti-over, dare base, leapfrog, crack-the-whip, and baseball. Every boy played on the baseball teams because there were only 12 to 15 boys in all eight grades. No girls were allowed. The little kids played the outfield and the bigger ones the infield. When I got older, I and my buddy, Albert Renterghem, had to be on opposite teams because we were the only two boys in our grade. New teams were chosen up every day. We tossed a bat up into the air and one captain caught it. He and the other captain then went hand over hand to the top of the bat and the last one to be able to hold onto the bat got first pick of the players. Our "baseball" was made of wrapped cotton twine, sewed to keep it together. There was one catcher's mitt with a hole in it, and one or two boys had a glove. I didn't. When I was younger and playing the outfield I got a bloody nose. A line drive was hit toward the outfield and I was going to catch it, but someone in front of me jumped and tipped it up and instead of going into my hands it hit me square on the nose.

After lunch and recess, the teacher called us back into the school house by ringing a school bell, a hand-held one, not a big church bell.

Typical School Bell

The girls joined the boys in dare base, anti-over, and occasionally crack-the-whip. Crack-the-whip was frowned upon by the teachers because the ones at the end of the tail would invariably get thrown down.

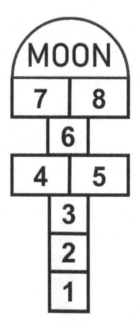

Hopscotch Diagram

The girls also played hopscotch. In this game a diagram consisting of eight squares and a half-moon was marked out. One tossed a stone into a square and then hopped on one leg sequentially through the squares, skipping the one containing one's stone, over the moon, and then back down the squares, picking up one's stone on the way. The stone started at square one and proceeded through all eight squares. Failure to toss one's stone on the proper square, failing to maintain the one-legged stance, stepping on one's own square, or stepping out of a square put one out of the game.In the wintertime when the weather was really bad we stayed inside. At these times we played Pin the Tail on the Donkey, flew paper airplanes, or spun tops. At first, the planes were made like regular airplanes, with wings sticking straight out of the sides. I got the idea of folding the paper so that the wings were nothing but triangles and that's the way they were made after that.

String-Wound Top, Ready to Throw

Tops were spun by throwing them upside down and yanking back on a string wrapped around them. The string had a loop around a ring at the top of the top and this, at the last moment, yanked the top upright so it spun on its point. With this type of throwing, about the only contest there could be was whose top spun the longest. I came up with a way to throw the top in an upright position and we could then try to hit the top of another's top.

There also were some card games. One I remember being played was Pitch. I never learned how and never participated.

We had every Friday afternoon free of classes. Then we would do "fine arts," such as singing, embroidery (oh yes, the boys embroidered too), spelling bees, arithmetic matches, rhythm band, or play practice. I have a dresser scarf with 450 French knots that I did for Mom. She used it until it began to fall apart. A favorite embroidery task was taking dishtowels made from flour sacks and embroidering a different design for each day of the week. I remember that Monday was washday. We always put on a variety "review" for Christmas. Short plays, poem readings, and the like.

One thing that is not done today is to make the pupils work at school. Every evening after school students sprinkled oiled sawdust on the floors and swept them. They also washed the blackboards (real slate) and dusted the erasers. This was a chore that was rotated so that everyone got a turn. It was the eighth grade boys' job to keep the stove fired when it was a one-room school, and the furnace after we had two rooms. In later years, my brother Al got paid a few cents to walk to school early and fire up the furnace.

When I first started school, we had desks of the type shown below, but we didn't have slates like those shown. There were two kinds of desks, one-seaters and two-seaters. They were mounted on two-by-fours so that they could be lined up front-to-back with an even spacing. Each desk had an ink well, but I don't remember ever using one. The tops were hinged and we stored our books under the tops. Later we got more modern desks, but I don't recall when.

School Desks Similar to Ours

When I got out of the second grade, my dad and Louis Hoelscher, both directors of the school district, built a second room, with a wood-fired furnace, onto the school. They then set out to hire a second teacher. I accompanied Dad when he went to see Emma Hazelhorst about continuing to teach in the school. Dad had to inform her that new state regulations required that she attend summer school at Warrensburg State Teachers College. She said she could not afford to do that and would have to give up teaching. Another good teacher succumbed to bureaucracy. Dad then hired Delphine and Jeraldine Huhmann, distant relatives of Mom's, from Meta, Missouri.

Having two teachers made the teaching much easier. Earlier, Emma Hazelhorst had taught the first and second graders separately and taught combined classes made up of third and fourth graders, fifth and sixth graders, and seventh and eighth graders. With two teachers, the lower grade teacher only taught three classes and the upper grade teacher taught only two. One year, for instance, sixth grade subjects would be taught collectively to the fifth and sixth graders and the next year fifth grade subjects. It was possible to be in a class one year and back up a class the next year. We had penmanship classes (writing) in the early grades, reading, arithmetic, geography, and history. When I first started, reading was taught through all eight grades, but by the time I hit fifth grade, it was dropped for the upper grades, since we now had social studies which was supposed to give us enough reading practice. I think that was the beginning of the end, since school now seems more devoted to teaching social skills than it is to teaching basics.

I got in trouble with the two Huhmann girls over a problem that Dad had seen. It involved the use of a board and the weighing of two pigs. The question was what was the weight of the pigs. The teachers worked all one lunch period on the problem without getting the answer. After lunch I opened my big mouth to say that my dad knew the answer. To this one of the teachers replied that if my dad was so smart why wasn't he down there teaching school. Of course, with my big mouth, I relayed this to Dad that evening and caught more hell because of my smart mouth.

Our library consisted of one storage cabinet full of books covering material from first grade to eighth grade. This included the encyclopedias and dictionaries. I had read every book in the library, including the encyclopedias, long before I reached eighth grade. Fortunately, Father Oligschlager had arrived and he set up a library in the rectory. We had lots of free time while another class was being taught, and I don't believe I ever had to take any homework home.

As the area was almost 100 percent Catholic, most of the kids attended Mass each morning after which we received religious instruction from the pastor. After that we would all run down to the school. One morning, Irvin Hoelscher, stumbled and fell on the gravel which covered the east school grounds and hit his head. He embedded a stone in his forehead and carries the resulting scar to this day.

When my brother Clarence got out of the eighth grade, he had to live in Jefferson City, working at St. Mary's Hospital for his room and board, so he could go to high school there. Missouri law required only eight grades of education or attendance up to 14 years of age. Our district had no high school and wasn't required to pay for any high school education.

This living away from home was followed by my brother Roderick and myself, as well as a number of cousins.

I worked in the pharmacy and on the second floor (the men's floor) of the hospital when I was there the first year. In the pharmacy work, I unpacked all the medicines received, delivered medicine to each floor, and measured out two gallons of alcohol, one isopropyl and one medicinal (drinkable.) One time I came to work after school to find that the U.S. Inspector had been there and found that according to our records, we had 11 gallons too much medicinal alcohol in our barrel. This was next to a crime because, being used for medicinal purposes, the alcohol was not taxed. After that we had to record every ounce that we used.

The second year, I also worked in the kitchen for Sister Bertina, a little Polish nun. She seemed to thoroughly dislike me while she adored my brother Rod. She was always claiming that I didn't dry the pots well, didn't wash the walk-in coolers well (an every morning before school job.) However, I think much of this was a bluff to keep me on my toes. Every evening she would give us a quart of ice cream and a large bottle of soda. We always caught hell about the soda bottles because we would forget to return them and Sister Caroline, who was in charge of the "Boy's House," would complain to Sister Bertina.

Sister Bertina was "old country" born (Poland) and bred and loved to haggle with merchants. Her favorite was Mr. Mercurio who ran a grocery store and sold her produce and the like. When he showed up, Sister Bertina would put on her armor and declare that the tomatoes, corn, potatoes, or whatever he sold her the last time were half rotten or shriveled or some such (untrue of course) and she wasn't going to buy any more. He would bristle up and claim that he only sold her the best and they would haggle back and forth until he finally apologized for any produce that was bad the last time and avow that it wouldn't happen again. Then she would give in and order what she needed.

Thursday night (after all our other work was done) was the night to scrub the hospital halls. This included hand scrubbing the wall bases which were made of marble tile. The men who worked at the hospital full time helped with this.

I roomed in the Boy's House on the third floor with my brother Roderick, cousin Frank Braun, and Jerome "Jerry" Schmidt, later a renowned urologist. We all had a hard time waking up, especially Jerry. He rigged a hand wind alarm clock with an electrical switch which was activated by the alarm winder when the alarm went off. This switch operated a large bell which would set up an awful clatter. We, however, often did not hear it and would be awakened by one of the men who resided a floor below hammering on our door.

We were not without our tricks. A favorite was to take a towel, place it in a sink with a surgical glove on top of it and fill the glove with water. The glove would expand to fill the whole sink. We would tie it off and carry it on the towel to the room of one of the men and carefully place it under the covers on the bed and roll it off the towel. If the occupant tried to lift it with his hands it would burst and flood his bed. Gaining access to any room was a snap because any of the locks could be easily picked. Another trick was to wait until someone was in the shower and then flush all the toilets and turn on the cold water taps. The shower water would become boiling hot. After many curses and shouts from the shower taker we would then reverse the process, turning on all the hot water taps. Then of course we would run like hell for our digs and lock the door.

One time one of us went to the railroad roundhouse and lifted some "torpedoes" from a hand car. These were made to be strapped to a track, and when a train went over them, would explode with enough noise for the engineer of a steam engine to hear them and read the code pattern laid out on the track. We got a length of pipe, a bolt to stick in one end, and a dowel pin to put in the other end of the pipe. We taped a torpedo over the bolt and climbed to the roof of the hospital and dropped it four stories by the front office window.

It went off with a satisfying bang. We retrieved the gadget and repeated the process, this time off the back of the hospital between two wings. Because of the semi-enclosed space the bang was enormous and people in the houses a street away came out on their front porches and shouted to one another about it. We heard and saw this and skedaddled down the fire escape to the Boy's

House and disposed of the evidence. Fortunately, it was dark and we weren't seen. We then went back to the hospital to "investigate" the commotion. Both the Highway Patrol and Jefferson City police were there and we wondered with them what had caused the loud noise. We then went down to the kitchen and discovered that Sister Bertina had been carrying a dishpan of tomatoes past the window where the torpedo went off. She had thrown the pan up in the air and scattered tomatoes everywhere. We helped her pick them up and she rewarded us with another quart of ice cream.

In my last year at the hospital, Jerry Schmidt and I set up in the business of operating on rabbits. Jerry worked in the hospital laboratory and part of his job was taking care of the rabbits and guinea pigs used for tests. One test using rabbits was a pregnancy test. The rabbit was injected and after a few days was killed and its ovaries examined to determine whether the woman was pregnant. Jerry convinced the nun in charge of the laboratory that money could be saved if he and I operated on the rabbits instead of killing them. In this way they could be reused. We would be paid

$2.50 for each rabbit operation. We made an operating table of plywood. I was the anaesthesiologist and Jerry did the actual operation with me handing him instruments and holding the incision open with forceps. Our first one, after a few days, began to drag its legs. Of course we used the autopsy table, killing it first with an injection of air in a vein, to examine it for the cause. It had gotten peritonitis.

The hospital underwent a building program that added a wing and Sister Bertina's "cellar," an enormous room, had to be moved. We discovered bottles of wine that Sister Bertina had made in 1927, the first year she was there, and forgotten. She gave them to us boys and we strained the sediment out of them with gauze from the emergency room and drank it. The room also contained forgotten sacks of dried apples and boxes of pudding, all of which the good sister gave to my parents to feed their hungry mob.

I was a junior when my uncle Frank got a job in Jefferson City at Montgomery Ward and I and my cousin Anstine rode into town and back home with him. In the wintertime he had to get into Jefferson City by 5:30 a.m. to get the furnace going so we had to get up very early then. The store closed at 5:30 p.m. while school was out at 2:30 p.m. so we had all afternoon to while away. I used this time to wander around the county courthouse, the county library, the city library, the supreme court, and the highway patrol headquarters.

I am proud to say that our one and, later, two-room school turned out teachers, engineers, doctors, and nurses, as well as successful farmers.

World War II

I WON'T ATTEMPT to do justice to World War II, but I will tell a few things about it. Contrary to popular belief, none of us remembered where we were when Pearl Harbor was attacked. In fact, we didn't know about it for a few days because we had no newspaper and no radio at the time.

My uncle, Clement Mertens, was one of the first to be inducted in the Army. He trained at Jefferson Barracks in St. Louis and my mom and dad drove down one time to visit him there. He later went out to California and eventually wound up in charge of the Mess Hall for the entire LeMoore Army Air Corps base. He got citations for his marksmanship and it was easy to see why. When he came to our place on furlough he would take our .22 caliber single-shot rifle and shoot empty shell casings off the top of our wash line posts.

Clem got to come back to Missouri one time from California to pick up an AWOL soldier from Kentucky or Tennessee. He carried a .45 in a holster then. He told us that if his prisoner escaped, he himself would have to serve out the prisoner's sentence.

During the war, coffee, sugar, gasoline, tires, shoes, etc. were rationed. This hit us hard in that we canned most of our food and needed sugar for that. People who lived in the cities could buy their canned fruit and jelly with sugar already in it and could use their sugar ration for other things. There were A and B ration cards for gasoline. Ours was the lowest. I don't know how many gallons of gasoline we got but I know it wasn't much and pleasure driving was definitely out. Because of the coffee shortage, we began to use two substitutes for drinking, Postum and Ovaltine. Postum was made from burned bran and tasted sort of like coffee, but had no caffeine. Ovaltine was a chocolate tasting drink made with hot water.

The war boosted the economy and was what

eventually ended the Great Depression, especially on the farm. Life went on essentially as it always had except for those who had men in the service. My dad was 40 and had six children, but would have been drafted had he not been deferred because he was a farmer. Leo Hofer was 45 and a bachelor and was drafted. He didn't like it and managed to get a dishonorable discharge through various shenanigans. My classmate Albert Renterghem's brother, Joe, was drafted and drove a tank. He was the only man from our area to die in the war. One of the Siebeneck boys was shot in the knee.

The Stores

THE TWO MAIN STORES that figured in our lives were the one at Osage Bend and the one at Osage Bluff. When I could remember it, the one at Osage Bend was owned by Leo Bisges. We usually visited it on Sunday morning after Mass because it was just across the road from the church. Like all the other buildings in the "town" it was covered with tin that simulated stone. It had a main central part that contained the main store, a room on the west that held sacked grain and other such supplies, and a complete two story house on the east. When I was going to school, the school teachers rented rooms in the house and lived there. Very convenient, less than a block from the school. Leo, his wife, Regina, and their young children lived in the rest of the house.

There was a gasoline pump on the west side next to a big persimmon tree. On Sunday, no one parked under the persimmon tree. That spot was reserved for John Schmidt and his family who came to church in a horse-drawn buggy. John always tied his horse to the tree. It was in the late 1930s when John finally gave in and bought a Model T Ford touring car with snap on sides. One of John's sons, Jerome, a good friend of mine, went on to become a noted urologist in Jefferson City, Missouri and only recently retired.

When Grandma stayed with us, we often walked down to the store in the summer time to buy #16 thread for her overall patching. We, of course, also bought a box of oatmeal or a sack of puffed wheat for 16¢. A 50-pack of 0.22 caliber rifle shells cost 50¢. We never bought much at Bisges' store, but reserved most of our purchases for Emil Hirschman's store at Osage Bluff.

Emil Hirschman's store at Osage Bluff was a stopping point when we came back home from a trip to Jefferson City. Dad would buy three gallons of gasoline which cost 50¢. The gasoline was pumped up from underground by working a lever side-to-side on the side of the gas pump.

The gas pump stood about eight feet tall and had a cylindrical glass container at the top which held ten gallons. The container would be pumped over full and the excess was allowed to drain back underground. As it drained back, the level in the glass would lower until the zero gallon mark would be reached. As the gas reached this mark and fell just below that, the surface tension holding the gas under the mark would let go and a small wave would ripple across the glass cylinder. The hose nozzle was then stuck in the gas filler on the car and a lever pulled allowing the gas to enter the car's tank. When the gas reached the exact level of gallons bought, a wave would ripple across the gas cylinder and the hose would then be shut off. Gasoline was always bought by the gallon, not by dollar amount.

Emil Hirschman's store was about 40 feet long and about 40 feet wide. A room about 15 feet wide was walled off on the east side with a back door that led to it and to a stairway to the second floor. There also was a door to the outside front from this room. The remaining store area was devoted to everyday sales with counters on both sides almost the length of the store. In the back right was a door that led to Emil Hirschman's house. There was a concrete walkway between the store and the house, one of the few concrete walks in the whole area.

About half-way toward the rear of the store was a long wood stove that heated the place in the winter. Men from the neighborhood would congregate around the stove in the winter and swap tales till late evening. I believe Emil closed the store around 10 o'clock at night. At the right hand side was the main counter where Emil wrapped the goods and totted up the sale. The cash register stood on a shelf behind the counter and was completely mechanical. When sales were rung up, metal tags with the sales price would rise up in a glassed-in area at the top of the register. After electricity came through there was a beer and soda cooler near the front by this counter. I might add that most items were wrapped in brown paper and tied with string. The brown paper was on a large roll on the counter and the string was in a big ball enclosed in an iron cage that hung from the ceiling.

Further down the counter was the candy display in front of which we kids would park ourselves and stare as though we were starving. I guess Emil felt sorry for us, because after Dad and Mom had made their purchases, he would take a small paper sack and put some candy in it and give it to us kids.

Emil sold practically anything. There were canned goods, staples like sugar, salt, and coffee, bib overalls, shoe buttons although no one wore them anymore, dynamite, vinegar, clothing dyes, fishing tackle, horse harnesses, lamp wicks and chimneys, chicken feed, gasoline, and cow feed. He sold rifle bullets, rivets, nails, candy, and matches. The chicken feed came in decorative sacks that the women used to make dresses and blouses. They would check over Emil's supply and pick out the proper feed sack to match one they already had or a pattern that they liked and that often required Emil to move a lot of sacks to get to the particular one wanted.

I would always stop by the store when we came back from Philadelphia on vacation and talk with Emil and his wife, Paula. They seemed as proud of each of our children as we were. One time, Emil said to me, "Py Gott Qvuentin, vat iss goink on? A couple of FBI men stopped here to ask about you." I had to tell Emil that that was standard practice when one was getting Secret clearance for government work.

Emil would buy and sell eggs, beer, and soda. He also bought cattle. I remember he and Dad bargaining over a cow and a calf that Emil finally bought for $17.50. He also bought small pigs from us for $10 a piece one time.

I don't know if he extended credit to everybody, but I do know that he extended it to Dad. The bill at one time got as high as $80, a big amount during the Depression.

The Parish Picnic

BEFORE I WAS BORN, the Parish of St. Margaret held annual picnics which were attended by people from the surrounding communities. About the time I was born, a new pastor, Father Wagner, came to replace Father Denner. Father Wagner did not get along with the church trustees who at that time were a powerful group. The parish split into factions and the annual picnic was dropped. When Father Ohligschlager replaced Father Wagner, the parish picnic was brought back to life.

Father Ohligschlager bought two veal calves which he fed to butchering size on the church grounds. These were butchered and furnished the beef for the picnic supper. Father Ohligschlager talked Dad into donating 110 posts to fence in the parish grounds so he could pasture the beef. Before it was fenced in, the parish grounds were part of our school playground since they were just across the road from the school. The parishioners donated a number of chickens which were butchered at one of the farms before the picnic. There must have been about 150 to 200 chickens. The kids got to help with cutting off the chickens' heads and plucking the feathers. The women did the disemboweling and cutting up of the chickens.

The day before the picnic, the grounds were set up. This involved setting up tables and chairs in the old hall, building booths, and setting up the chicken frying stoves. These stoves were wood-fired and about ten of them were set up on the west side of the hall. The women fried the chicken in regular skillets and kept the fried chicken warm in the ovens. A number of kids were assigned to firing up the stoves. My mother was one of the chicken fryers. I often wondered how many chickens each cook fried. We served upwards of 1,000 dinners. I wasn't in on the butchering of the beef so I don't know how that was done or how the beef was cooked. Nowadays each family takes home several beef roasts and cooks them before the picnic and the chicken is bought already cut up and packed in ice. The cooked roasts are brought to the picnic grounds the morning of the picnic and sliced with an electric slicer. There must be quite a variety of cooked beef at today's picnics.

Every family donated corn, potatoes, green beans, tomatoes, etc., to supply the necessary vegetables. They also donated home-made bread which was the only kind served. Older kids were assigned to wait on the tables and pour water and iced tea. An adult poured the hot coffee.

There was quite a variety of booths at the picnic. One favorite was the penny pitch. This consisted of a large flat table at ground level with squares marked with different monetary values, in cents of course. One pitched a penny and tried to get it to land exactly on one of the squares. If it did, the pitcher got the number of pennies indicated by the square. There was a "kitty" in the center of the board into which pennies could slide. It was glass covered and had a one dollar bill taped under the glass. If your penny landed exactly on George Washington's face without touching one of the edges, you got the dollar plus whatever pennies had slid into the kitty. It was a popular game.

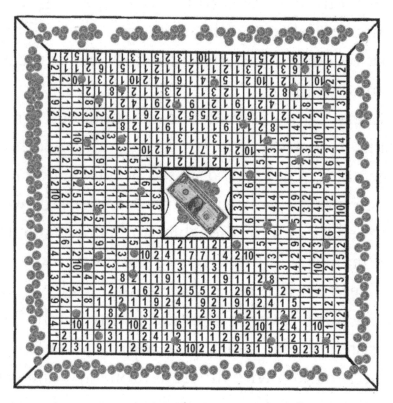

Penny Pitch Game Board

Another game of skill was the cane toss. Here a bunch of "canes" were lined up in a net and the object was to toss a ring and have it go around one of the canes and thereby win the cane. Most of the canes were "garden variety," just a lathe-turned head and a quarter-inch dowel for the main part. The canes were brightly colored and every child wanted to get at least one. This was not easy because the rings just fit around the cane heads and usually just bounced off when they were thrown. There were some fancy canes in the group with a dog head or the head of a person. These were a prize much sought after. A few of the ordinary canes had a small pen knife or other gewgaw taped to the cane.

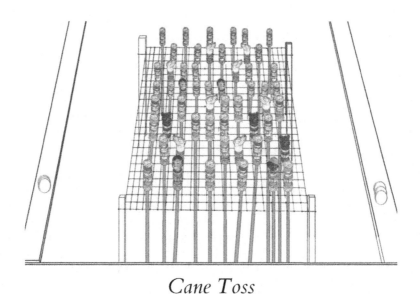

Cane Toss

Another game quite popular with the young kids was the fish pond. I don't know why it was called that since there was neither fish nor a pond. A child paid his or her money and held the fish pole over the top of the booth. An unseen attendant attached a bag with a prize to the string. Of course the attendant had a peep hole and could select the prize according to the gender of the player.

The beer stand was very popular. All the beer was in bottles and included such brands as Miller's, Alpenbrau, Griesedieck, Old Milwaukee, Busch, Capitol City, Falstaff, etc. Much of the beer was consumed away from the stand so the grounds were littered with empty bottles. This was a source of money for small kids who went around with empty cases collecting the empty bottles and getting a few pennies in return from the men running the beer stand.

There was a separate ice cream and soda stand. My dad usually ran this. Today, the stand only dispenses soda from pressurized cans. In my day, all the soda was in bottles and was kept in large coolers and covered with ice. We had Royal Crown, many flavors of Vess such as grape, cream, or strawberry, Coca Cola, 7-Up, Dr. Pepper, etc. Workers in the stand had to memorize where each flavor was in the coolers and pick the right one out of the ice water. Picnic day was usually hot and this created a danger with the soda bottles. Every now and then, when a hot bottle was placed in the cooler it would explode and there was broken glass to be fished out of the water.

We sold three flavors of ice cream scooped out of big containers and served in baked cones. There were no ice cream bars or other such innovations. My dad would buy a big bunch of bananas and these were sold for a dime apiece and were great favorites. Empty soda bottles were collected just like the empty beer bottles.

We had a makeshift bowling setup which was very popular. It consisted of two wooden lanes that were made of tongue and grooved boards nailed to two-by-fours in three or four sections. These were set side by side with a ball return in the middle. The ball return consisted of boards nailed in a "V" shape with a slope from the back of the alley to the front. The alleys were not "normal" in that they were wider by two boards where the pins were set, making it almost impossible to get a lone seven or ten pin. At the rear of the alley there was a rank of straw bales to stop the balls. After two balls were thrown, the pins were set up by hand by a teenage kid. The balls would be tossed into the v-shaped return and would go sailing down to a pen near where the bowler stood. There was a variety of balls, some with two finger holes, some with three, and some with none. The ones with none were generally smaller balls. The player paid a dime and got to bowl two balls. If he got a strike, he won a cigar. If he got a spare, he got to bowl another game. It was fun to watch a "city" bowler bowling on the lanes for the first time. The alleys were elevated by the height of a two-by-four and the bowler stood at ground level. The first time a "city" bowler would bowl, he invariably hit the end of the alley with the ball and shocked his fingers. He soon learned the alley was higher than the approach.

There was a bingo booth which was run differently than at present. No money was given out to the winner. Instead, the winner was allowed to select from a display of prizes. Uncle Frank was in charge of this booth and he had quite a task, selecting and buying all the different prizes. The prizes were not junk. One time I won and got a neat table lamp as the prize. Another time I got a galvanized pan for draining engine oil. In the early days, cardboard cards were used with grains of corn being used as markers. Later we graduated to using cards with sliding windows.

The grounds were lighted with electric lights strung between the trees. At first, the electricity was supplied by a gasoline engine driving a Delco generator with a 24-volt storage battery that was huge. The generator was housed in a wooden shed between the hall and the church. Surprisingly, there was no electricity connected to the church. It was lit by oil lamps until the REA brought electricity to the area.

Some people had these types of generators and had electric lights. My uncle Rudolph was one of them. However, I never saw his lights used.

After serving of dinners was finished, there was a mad rush to clean up the hall to put away the tables and chairs so that a dance could be held in the hall at 9 o'clock. Admission to the dance was 50 cents. The music was furnished by a local western music band, often the C&O boys, consisting of Alfred Schmidt, Alvin Schmidt, Dick Schroeder, and some others. The dance lasted until 12 a.m., at which time "Home Sweet Home" was played, signaling the end of the dance. All the booths remained open and the grounds were full of people until the dance ended.

Afterword

SO I HOPE YOU ENJOYED your visit to Osage Bend! It's one of my favorite places in the world, and I still make it a point to attend the annual church picnic every summer. You should come some time—the food is fantastic!

In the next section is the author biography, and I'd just like to add a few things to it (my dad wrote most of it himself, so it's not nearly flattering enough!)

My dad was truly what they call a "Renaissance Man". He was an electrical engineer by profession, and at the time of his retirement was considered one of the top engineers at McDonnell Douglas (now Boeing). But he was also a talented writer, as you've just experienced yourself. He was a proficient handyman around the house, and good with all kinds of DIY projects. He was interested in all kinds of things, from astronomy to religion to politics to genealogy, and our home was always filled with books.

But most of all, Dad was a people person. He was the person you went to when you needed advice, or just someone to talk to. He could relate to anyone, from the most intellectual to the tiniest child. He never condescended, even though he was way smarter than almost anyone else. People he worked with came to him with their personal as well as work problems. We kids came to him for help with homework, as well as heartbreaks. Either way, he always listened, and always made it better.

Of course, of all people, family came first with Dad. He loved his parents, his siblings, our mom, us kids, his grandchildren. We spent all our holidays and summer vacations at the farm, getting to spend time with our grandparents, aunts, uncles, and cousins. Not to mention getting to know the workings of a farm—although it was much different in my childhood than in this book. By the time I came along, the farm had electricity and indoor plumbing. The brooder house was our clubhouse. While some of my older cousins helped with the haying, the barn and hayloft was a playhouse, where my cousins, siblings and I built "houses" out of hay bales and played school.

Grandma made us go to Mass and do some chores, along the lines of feeding the chickens and peeling potatoes, but nothing like the chores my dad did just to help the family survive when he was young. It certainly makes me appreciate all the conveniences we take for granted now, when reading about the way it was back then.

We lost my dad way too soon, and we still miss him every day. Working on this book has been bittersweet for me. As I read, I can hear his voice telling the story, and it makes me miss him even more. But I'm happy to be able to share his stories with other readers, and I know it would make him happy too. Love you, Dad!

Janice (Veit) Vail
April, 2020

Author Biography

QUENTIN VEIT was born on October 21, 1931 in a small farmhouse about one and one-half miles from Osage Bend, Missouri on the Osage Bluff road. He was the son of Clarence Albert Veit and Anna Frances Mertens. Quentin attended the Osage Bend public school for eight years, the first two years with only one teacher for all eight grades. After graduating from the eighth grade at the Osage Bend school, Quentin attended St. Peter High School in Jefferson City, Missouri, where the girls were taught by the School Sisters of Notre Dame and the boys were taught by Christian Brothers.

During his first two high school years Quentin worked for his room and board at St. Mary's Hospital in Jefferson City. This was his only way to obtain a high school education because the Osage Bend School District did not have a high school and would not pay for a high school education outside the district. Missouri law then required school attendance only until graduation from eighth grade or the age of 14, whichever came sooner.

During his last two high school years, Quentin commuted from Osage Bend with his uncle, Frank Veit, who had begun working for Montgomery Ward Store in Jefferson City. Quentin was editor of the Scroll, the high school's newspaper, and co-editor of the school's yearbook in 1949.

He graduated as valedictorian of his class in 1949, receiving a tuition-only scholarship to St. Louis University in St. Louis, Missouri. That summer, Quentin worked on his dad's farm putting up hay, working on the threshing run, and plowing with horses for the fall wheat sowing. Quentin studied electrical engineering at St. Louis University for two years, working in the University Library during his freshman year and working in a service station at night during his sophomore year. In between his freshman and sophomore years, Quentin again worked on the farm and also helped his dad build a home in Jefferson City for Quentin's brother Roderick and his wife Rose.

That same year Quentin met his future wife, Joyce Willett, at a dance in Jefferson City. In the summer after his sophomore year, Quentin and his dad built a house on Swifts Highway in Jefferson City for Al Kroeger, whose daughter later married one of Quentin's nephews.

Living expenses in St. Louis had become too high and so Quentin transferred to the Engineering School at the University of Missouri at Columbia, Missouri for his junior year. During the week he lived with his uncle and aunt, Clement and Ida Mertens, at Columbia. On weekends he took a bus to Jefferson City and then hitched a ride home to Osage Bend. He worked with his dad on Saturdays doing carpenter work for the grand wage of $1.25 per hour. This paid his two-way bus fare, his $5.00 per week room and board bill to his aunt and uncle, and left a little extra for incidental expenses.

The following summer Quentin took a job in St. Louis, Missouri as an inspector of automatic screw machine parts with White Rodgers Electric, maker of furnace controls. During the next college term Quentin lived at home in Osage Bend and commuted daily to and from Columbia for classes, riding to Jefferson City with his uncle Frank Veit in the morning, riding from Jefferson City to Columbia and back with a distant relative, Bill Taube, who commuted from Taos, Missouri, and riding from Jefferson City to home with his dad in the evenings.

The following summer, on June 6, 1953, Quentin married Joyce Willett at Annunciation Catholic Church in California, Missouri. The couple then moved to St. Louis where they both worked for McDonnell Aircraft Company, Joyce in the Personnel Department and Quentin in Flight Testing as a "Summer Engineering Intern." That fall Quentin and Joyce moved to Columbia, where Quentin attended the fall term to make up class credit he had lost in the transfer between schools. Quentin graduated from the University of Missouri with a Bachelor of Science Degree in Electrical Engineering in February 1954.

Upon graduation, he immediately went to work in Philadelphia, Pennsylvania for Philco Corporation, makers of radios, televisions, refrigerators, military electronics, and industrial communications equipment. Quentin worked in Philco's industrial half of the Government and

Industrial Division, first as an electronics design engineer and later as an engineering supervisor until October of 1963. At that time Quentin and Joyce, with their family of seven children, moved to Florissant, Missouri when Quentin went to work for the Electronic Equipment Division of McDonnell Aircraft Company. Quentin spent the next 28 years at McDonnell, which later became present-day Boeing, designing and supervising the design of advanced electronic equipment, mostly for aircraft use.

By the time Quentin retired in October 1991, he and Joyce numbered among their descendants nine children, all with college degrees. Quentin and Joyce also had 30 grand- and step-grandchildren, one of whom is deceased. They also had two great-grandchildren.

Quentin had always been interested in family history and began his genealogical research in the mid-1960s. Due to the time pressures of raising a large family and working (with much overtime), it wasn't until 1988 that he was able to finally publish his first book, entitled *Willett Family History*. With his brother Albert, Quentin then co-authored *Joseph Veit and Francisca Scholz* (published in 1994) and *The William Hopen Clan of Missouri* (published in 1998.) In 2002, Quentin published *History of Henry Joseph Mertens and his wife Maria Magdalena Loethen*. In addition to the family history, this book contained 23 appendices with supplemental information, including this book, originally called *The Way it Was*.

Quentin developed heart problems and passed away suddenly in June 2004 due to an unfortunate reaction to medication used to treat his condition. He is still greatly missed.

A Note *from the* Editor

Dear Reader,

Thank you for taking the time to read *The Bumpy Road*. It has truly been a joy to edit this book and make it publicly available. Although the author, my father, wrote this over 20 years ago, it was recently rediscovered by my sisters and me. Reading Dad's stories gave me a sense of awe and pride, plus a few chuckles. I will always be grateful to him, not only for leaving us this written legacy, but for being such an amazing person and father.

I hope you enjoyed *The Bumpy Road*. If so, I'd appreciate if you left a review on Amazon. Reviews help other readers decide to try out a new book. Just a sentence or two saying what you liked about the book will do!

I'd like to acknowledge my sisters, Janice Vail and

Mary Verner, for collaborating with me on this project. Thanks to both of you for your hard work in converting the original documents and photos, proofreading, and helping to organize the material into its current form.

Ellen M. (Veit) Meyer
May, 2020

Table of Illustrations

Photo Credits

As many of the original photos and sketches as possible have been included in this book. The sketches were hand-drawn by the author, sometimes from scale models that he built himself, and these are irreplaceable. But in some cases, the original images were not available to include in this publication. Where possible, I have substituted comparable images and photographs that illustrate the same equipment and tools as those which appeared in the original version.

Most of the new images are in the public domain. The exceptions are credited below.

1. Ole Barney, *1932 Model B Ford Like Ours*. By Lglswe - Own work, CC BY-SA 3.0, https://commons.wikimedia.org/w/index.php?c urid=9728909
2. Grandpa and Grandma Veit, *Grape and Cider Press Like Grandpa Veit's*. Junior apple cider press photo by Loretta Sorensen,

https://www.farmcollector.com/equipment/anti
que-cider-presses-zm0z12octzbea

3. Neighborhood Cooperatives, *Threshing Machine*. By Bill Burris - Flickr: Threshing machine, CC BY-SA 2.0, https://commons.wikimedia.org/w/index.php?c urid=11340530

4. Neighborhood Cooperatives, *Hand-Operated Water Pump*. By Hisahiro Liu - Own work, CC BY-SA 3.0, https://commons.wikimedia.org/w/index.php?c urid=16280070

Made in the USA
Monee, IL
13 December 2020

The Bumpy Road

Step back in time to the tiny farm community of Osage Bend, Missouri, circa 1930-1945...

Part memoir, part how-to manual, *The Bumpy Road* paints a vivid picture of life on the farm during the Great Depression. The author, recounting stories from his boyhood, brings to life the everyday trials and tribulations of his family and neighbors as they struggle to survive under daunting economic conditions. The hard work they put in was a given (to them), and their solutions to everyday problems were ingenious by necessity. And yet, they still found time to socialize and make the church the center of their lives. These tenacious people always looked to the future with hope and determination, and that comes shining through in this book. Depression-era, yes, depressing, no!

So, discover the many facets of running a farm, how chores were done, the importance of family, and the many things that tied the community together. Marvel at the strength and resourcefulness of these rural Missourians—and take some of that for yourself as we endure our own difficult times today.

Bonus: Includes photos and illustrations of farm tools, implements, and household items from the era, many of which you can now only find in museums.

Quentin F. Veit grew up on a farm in central Missouri during the Great Depression. An engineer by trade, he also had interests in wood-working, history, crafts, inventions, and more. He is the author of four family history books. His writings document geneology as well as the way of life from times gone by. Quentin and his wife, Joyce, raised nine children and had many grandchildren and great-grandchildren, all of whom enjoyed hearing stories about the past.

Willow Bend
PRESS

ISBN 9798650979043